BUFFETT
and Beyond

BUFFETT
and Beyond

SECOND EDITION

Uncovering the Secret Ratio for
Superior Stock Selection

DR. JOSEPH BELMONTE

WILEY

Library of Congress Cataloging-in-Publication Data:

Belmonte, Joseph.
   Buffett and beyond : uncovering the secret ratio for superior stock selection/Joseph Belmonte.—Second edition.
      pages cm
   Includes index.
   ISBN 978-1-118-95577-2 (hardback); ISBN 978-1-118-95578-9 (ePub); ISBN 978-1-118-95579-6 (ePDF)
   1. Investment analysis. 2. Securities. 3. Buffett, Warren. I. Title.
   HG4529.B45 2015
   332.63′22—dc23

                                                                                2014043906

This book is dedicated posthumously to Tom Barnes, chief engineer of the S.S. Yellowstone in 1978. Without him, I would not be here to write this book.

To those of you who insisted that I write this book. To my wife, Debby, who "forced" me to write the first edition and for Tula at Wiley who insisted I write this second edition.

To my wonderful family who always stood behind me. Always. I miss you, Dad.

And, of course, to both Jimmy and Warren Buffett. If you want to live life on the beach like Jimmy, you have to learn to invest like Warren.

Contents

Preface: From Then Until Now

The first edition of this book was written between 2003 and 2004. We had just gone through the great market advance of the late 1990s, with 1999 being the absolute best year for our stock selection method in my market history. The rest of the stock market also roared and soared. Everyone seemed to be an expert or at least had tips on the next stock that would gain 100 percent over the next six months. The Internet gave everyone free research on company data, and people quit their jobs to become day traders.

Then there was Warren Buffett. Many of the new brokers and new investment advisers of that time had never heard of him. To all the younger folks, he was a relic of the past. In the late 1990s, fundamental analysis was not important because everything went up in price. Then the bubble blew. The tech bubble began to break in 2000, and the culmination of the market decline took place in 2002. By then, billions of dollars had been lost, especially in those companies that had no earnings. Enron happened and stock analysts were exposed because of their conflicts of interest. Wealth managers began scratching their heads. What happened?

The market came back to life in 2003 with our model portfolio gaining a bit over 52 percent, doubling the S&P returns. During the next four years we saw a housing boom turn into a housing bubble followed by the eventual bubble burst in 2008. We are still feeling the effects of that disaster, and some folks will never recover as the market and housing prices declined 50 percent and more by the end of February 2009.

Even before the dust began to clear, Warren Buffett came to the forefront to help try and put a calm on the markets. There he was, buying various securities while blood was running in the streets. Helping to save good companies while their stock prices seemed to be going to zero was a Buffett specialty. We all prayed that Buffett would come through and help us as he had in the past and, yes, our prayers were answered.

As the dust settled, Buffett began to be sought after for investment advice once again. Of course, by this time, Buffett had already purchased what he needed for the next decade. Yes, buying growth stocks at a good value was coming back into style. The problem was that very few people really understood how Warren Buffett selected his stocks and even fewer had any clue whatsoever how he selected his all-important purchase price.

Even by 2015 many investors continued to stay away from the market and no longer had money to purchase real estate (at good or fair prices) due to losses in the stock market during the 2008 debacle. Those who stayed in the stock market to weather the 2008 storm (Buffett, myself, and those of you who read the first edition) are very happy we did. We already had the very best companies gracing our portfolios, and we relied on good, sound management to keep adding value to these companies even though their stock prices were falling. Always remember that during panic sell-offs, value and price diverge tremendously.

Portfolio Insurance

A very important addition to this second edition shows you how we generate cash when the market goes through one of its very nasty declines. It is called—yes, you guessed it—portfolio insurance. Portfolio insurance allows you to keep your portfolio value mostly intact during those adverse economic market cycles. When the insurance pays off, it pays off in cash. And it pays off in cash when you need it most in order to buy stocks at or near market bottoms.

A Dividend Income and Growth Portfolio

Another new addition to this second edition is developing a dividend income and growth portfolio using the Buffett and Beyond stock selection method. There are several chapters covering this topic, and it just may be the answer to your investment future. You *must* read these chapters.

Now that the investing world has regained some semblance of sanity after a rather nasty 10 years since our last edition, you'll find out why the timeliness of this book will be so very important to your financial future. This book will show you the little-known stock selection methods of Warren Buffett. In addition, this book will show you my latest research, which, in turn, will take you one very important step *beyond*.

Introduction:
A Sea Story

Luck: When Opportunity Meets Preparation

A sea story is a tale or a yarn. Something like one of those "fish that got away" stories. However, our tale actually does begin with a story about the sea.

This introduction is a short story in itself. It is the story of how I came into contact with a little-known type of accounting, which was developed for the sole purpose of determining the predictability (or not) of the future performance of a company.

Predictability of future performance is the Holy Grail of investing. After all, if we could predict future earnings reasonably well, we would be able to determine which stocks should grace our portfolio in order to outperform the market averages on a consistent basis over any multiple-year time period.

One try at predictability was developed by the accounting community, and it was called Clean Surplus Accounting. My doctoral dissertation (2002) was the very first attempt by anyone to statistically test this method as to predictability. To everyone's surprise in the academic community, the tests came out exceptionally well: well enough, in fact, to be put into practical use in which actual results mimicked the very positive test results.

With much coercion by several folks close to me, the first edition of this book was written shortly after the publication of the doctoral dissertation. During the ensuing 10 years, the track record for the method I was testing showed a doubling of the returns of the S&P. With much coercion by more folks, this second edition came along.

Clean Surplus Accounting had pretty much been lost since its possible beginnings in 1895, except for a few rare instances between then and now. The field of accounting just did not evolve in the direction of being able to provide much-needed predictability. It very well could have, but it didn't. Clean Surplus Accounting was designed to try and provide that predictability. Very few people are presently aware of how to apply a reliable method of predictability to the fundamental elements of a stock. Those very few people are a very small group of academics, a handful of practitioners, and our friend, Warren E. Buffett.

Luck

I would like to discuss the events that guided me to my discovery of Clean Surplus in the first place.

It was luck, of course. But the definition of "luck" is when opportunity meets preparation. Had I not been involved in researching Clean Surplus Accounting and also at the exact same time reading everything about Warren Buffett that I could find, I never would have figured out that Clean Surplus was used by the greatest investor ever. On with our sea story and the events that guided my discovery.

I began my postgraduate education late in life. I began a master's program in business and finance at the ripe old age of 48 or so. In my prior life, I had been a marine engineer, and over the course of 13 years I worked on ships sailing to far away places with strange-sounding names. During that time, I rose to the position of chief engineer. I was working on a ship carrying grain from the United States to the then Soviet Union, and our ship had just entered the Mediterranean Sea through the Strait of Gibraltar. My position on the ship at that time was first engineer, which is the position directly under the chief engineer.

I brought most of the engine crew up on deck to see the great Rock of Gibraltar, but it was not to be, as we were sailing directly into a huge fog bank. With much disappointment, we went back down into the engine room to continue with the day's work. Unknown to us at that moment, our ship was soon to be involved in a horrible collision with a Liberian freight ship headed in our direction.

Ah, the egos of the men in positions of power are all too great. Which ship would give way to the other? Which ship would lose 20 minutes to avoid a collision at sea? Of course, neither one. That's why we were involved in a collision.

The approaching ship smashed into us in our rear port (left) side. Our ship was constructed with the engine room aft (in the rear of the ship). Since we were loaded with cargo and sat deep in the water, and the other freighter was light in the water, the other ship shattered the hull of our ship like paper and smashed into the engine room just above our heads, where I was working with most of the engine gang.

The engine room lights went out as an immense wall of water, as well as the bow of the other ship, entered our workspace. I found myself trapped in the engine room of a sinking ship quickly filling with water. The lights were extinguished immediately due to the entering seawater short-circuiting the electric panels. This left the entire engine room totally in the dark as we were being thrown about like paper dolls on a gigantic ocean wave.

If it hadn't been for the quick thinking of the chief engineer, Tom Barnes, this book never would have been written. He was able to start the emergency generator, which is located in a separate space away from the engine room, in order to provide us with very limited lighting for an extra 60 seconds or so. This light, seemingly sent from heaven, would lead the way for some of the men fighting for their lives in the turbulent water, helping them to find their way out of what would become a watery grave for several of our friends.

Some men made it to safety and some didn't. Five men died prematurely due to the total negligence of the captains of both ships. Some men were saved due to the quick thinking of the chief engineer who was, of course, not in the engine room at the time, but was on deck and in a position to help save some of us who were otherwise sure to die. Now you know why this book is dedicated to the memory of Chief Engineer Tom Barnes.

As the engine room completely filled with water, even the emergency lights were soon extinguished. After what seemed an eternity of struggling and swimming, I could no longer hold my breath and began to suck in seawater. It was at that exact moment that my head popped through the surface to breathe in the sweet salt air. It was also then that I decided to change careers and leave the salty sea, where pirates don't plunder and cannons don't thunder anymore (thank you, Jimmy Buffett) and head back to my cabin by the lake in the mountains of the Hudson River Valley. But what was I to do with the rest of my life? I had the feeling this was the beginning of a real midlife crisis.

While sitting on my outside deck and looking at the peaceful lake and the *Wall Street Journal* (now there's an oxymoron), I figured I should be able to take all those little numbers and make "cents" out of them. After all, I was an engineer.

Engineering is probably where my quantitative ability was honed to a fine edge. Ok, I'm being a bit silly here, but engineers are supposed to walk, talk, and dream in numbers. And to a certain extent this is true. I would rather look at the bottom-line results of a company's performance than think about the qualitative reasons the company obtained those results.

By "qualitative," I mean the good things a company does for its workers, which really can't be measured or valued in dollars and cents. If you can't put a dollar value on certain aspects of a company's operations, then those aspects won't show up as value on an income statement or a balance sheet. It could be the quality of life in the workplace. It could be those special folks in positions of power that smile at you and pat you on the back when you do well and encourage you when you are mediocre. It could be the daycare center run by the company or the special perks such as free lunch or flextime schedules.

Qualitative aspects could be the brainpower and/or work ethic of the employees and employers. You certainly can't put that on the balance sheet. How about those few people who light up the room when they walk in and make everyone around them happy to be there? Go ahead, accountants and finance people; put a dollar value on that!

However, if you think about it, all those good things about a company will eventually flow to the bottom line. I guess when mom said, "It all comes out in the wash," when I was a kid, she meant for me to take note of the bottom-line numbers once I eventually learned to read. I always knew mom was a finance person at heart.

During the next 10 years, I made my living investing in both real estate and stocks. I found the key to performing well in the stock market was being able to consistently outperform the market averages. However, I found consistently beating the market to be very difficult indeed.

I learned about stocks by sitting in a broker's office for an entire year while trading my own account and learning all I could. I learned technical analysis, and I also learned to use covered option writing, which I use to this day.

My stock strategy was simple back then. Buy stocks in the Dow Jones Industrial average (all 30 of them) and sell covered calls on those securities. Yes, I had more than enough taxable, short-term gains. However, back then, before most of my college students were four years old, you could invest in real estate and have the paper losses such as depreciation from real estate or other business assets offset other gains such as income from stocks or even salary income from your job. It was a great world back then. Combining a stock portfolio with real estate was the perfect strategy. I did it, I loved it, and life was good. However, some good things eventually come to an end.

The Tax Reform Act of 1986 changed my world. It changed the way certain items were allowed to be written off against other income. For you young folks, before the Act, in addition to the real estate write-offs, you could also write off the interest from your car loan, credit card loans, and school loans to help offset the taxable income from your job. Uncle Sam said it was good to be in debt because you could use the write-offs against salary, which in turn would reduce your total tax liability. And if your real job was investing in stocks, which sometimes gave you short-term gains, then the write-offs from real estate as well as other write-offs mentioned earlier could offset the income from stocks.

But as I said, the Tax Act of 1986 changed all of that. Full-time investing just wasn't as much fun as before. I figured it was time to change careers once again, and thus began yet another midlife crisis.

After much thought, I felt it was time to begin preparation for the fulfillment of an obligation I imposed upon myself earlier in life. My commitment was to pass on the knowledge I learned in this world before I left this world.

A hippie friend of mine once warned me against dying an ego death. An ego death is the act of learning all your life and not passing that knowledge on to others. My obligation was definitely not to die an ego death. So, I felt I could fulfill my obligation by going back to school to teach for a while, and at the same time I would be able to show the academic world just how they should be teaching about the real world.

I thought I would begin my teaching career by drawing up an outline for the finest investment course that could possibly be devised. I then submitted it to the university geographically closest to me at the time. Not to embarrass me, they did mention it would be a wonderful course coming from a "practitioner," but I really needed to obtain a few more academic degrees in order to qualify as a university instructor. After all, I "only" possessed a bachelor of science in engineering and really, what did an engineer know about investing? They told me that if I were going to teach a course on investing, I really should possess a Ph.D. in finance or something of the sort. Well, I had nothing to do for the next 10 years, so I went back to school with all the kids.

Several years later, while I was at the end of the one-and-one-half-year master's program (which took me four years), I went to yet another ho-hum lecture on stock selection. Within the first two minutes of this seminar I really thought I'd found the Holy Grail. I felt I had discovered (come across, not discovered) a method that was so unique and so simple that I wondered why I never heard about it before. Even more bewildering was why I had never thought of this uncomplicated, straightforward method myself.

The problem was there was no name for this system, but who cared? I didn't need a name for a stock selection system that was much simpler and seemingly better than anything I had seen up to that time (and since).

I sat in front of my computer for the next four-and-a-half months formulating spreadsheets on the Dow 30 stocks. I tested this simple but common sense strategy in every way possible. I took into consideration those academic measures of risk, with strange sounding names such as "beta" and "standard deviation." I also tested the strategy on certain Dow stocks at market bottoms, at market tops and, yes, even market middles.

The Academic World

Allow me to explain something here, folks. The academic world is filled with egos. It is filled with a lot of very bright people, many of whom do not use common sense. After all, it takes a long time to earn a Ph.D. or doctoral degree. It takes so much time to get a Ph.D. or doctoral degree that there is little time left to gain real-world experience. But those who do have those academic designations and want to combine real-world experience with their teachings are left at the mercy of the academic system. They must obey the number one rule of the academic world: *Thou shalt not teach anything in the university system that students might find useful in real life.*

An economics professor once told me that things you can actually use in the real world should only be taught in technical schools and not at the university level. Hmm.

I read somewhere that Sam Walton, founder of Wal-Mart Stores, Inc., would not be allowed to teach at the university level because he didn't have the proper credentials (degree). Hey, Warren Buffett wouldn't be allowed a full-time job as a university instructor either because he doesn't have a Ph.D. Now tell me, are the rules of the academic world arcane and bewildering, or what?

Risk

There are two definitions of risk taught by the academics: Beta, which is a measure of how a stock moves relative to the market; and standard deviation, which is a measure of how a stock moves relative to its own past returns. These are very simple definitions. If you want the full definitions, just take a 16-week finance course.

Now let me explain my very own, real-life definition of risk. The market goes up, my stocks go up. The market goes down, my stocks go down. The market goes back up, and somehow my stocks forget to go back up. That, my dear friends, is risk.

It is really this type of risk that the method used in this book will help you avoid. It is this risk that Warren Buffett tries to avoid. It is this risk that can almost always be eliminated by using Clean Surplus Accounting and investing for the longer term. And talking about Clean Surplus

Accounting, let's finish up with our sea story so we can begin both this book and your education of selecting a superior performing portfolio.

The Doctoral Degree

After finishing the master's program, I finally entered a university in order to obtain my doctoral degree. During the doctoral program, one must find a suitable theme for his or her dissertation. The dissertation is like the final burst of glory at the end of a fireworks display. All coursework should be finished, and finally, this very huge research paper must be completed, accepted, and defended in front of a committee of Ph.D. and/or doctoral type of people who are there just to make sure you jump through all the hoops and whistle all the whistles. If it doesn't take a person two or three years to complete the dissertation, well, it probably isn't up to the expectations of the academic community. One of my professors told me his dissertation took him seven years to complete after all his coursework was finished.

Before we do go on, let me loosely define a few terms just for your own worldly knowledge. There is a difference between a Ph.D. degree and a doctoral degree. Of course, the academic world likes to confuse us common folk as they bestow the title of "Doctor" upon both of these academic degrees. In short, the Ph.D. develops the theoretical work, and the owners of the doctoral degree take that theory and attempt to put it into practical use. You can remember it this way: Next time you enter the hospital for a procedure, you want a doctor operating on you and not a Ph.D.

Are there Ph.D.-type people in the real world who transgress the boundary and go into business and the real world? Are there doctoral-type people who are just theoretical and not very practical? Of course.

In order to complete either a Ph.D. or doctoral program, the dissertation (which I just spoke about) must be undertaken and completed. The dissertation is based upon past research. In other words, there must be a foundation of research in your particular area of choice. It is upon this previous research that the author of the dissertation adds more testing and research. The purpose of the dissertation is to add to that already existing body of knowledge. Once completed, the author is considered a worldly expert in the subject of his or her dissertation. If the subject has not been researched by many people, then the author could very well be one of the very few people in the entire world who is an expert on the dissertation subject.

Why am I torturing you with all of this? Well, I wanted to develop my dissertation on the method (the "no-name" method) I was exposed to several years previously. The problem was I couldn't find a name for this method. And if you don't know what something is called, then you certainly cannot explore the past research.

Thank the heavens for computers. Present-day researchers no longer have to spend their entire lives in a musty university library cellar. One now sits in front of a computer for hours on end. Dressed in pajamas or sweats and armed with a cup of coffee, you now have access to most of the magazines of the world and all the academic writings from the academic journals of the world. You just keep typing in key words or phrases, and the amazing search engines will find the academic and non-academic articles that contain those key words or phrases. Yes, life was good once again.

Well, I think you know where I'm going with this. I finally found a subject name for the method I wanted to research. It was called Clean Surplus Accounting. The first academic research article I found was written by James Ohlson (1989) of Columbia University in New York.

Well, dear reader, do you know who else attended Columbia University? Our very own hero, Mr. Warren E. Buffett, the greatest investor ever. And do you know whom he studied under while at Columbia University? Mr. Benjamin Graham, the "Father of Security Analysis."

Do these guys have a sort of club down (up, over) there? We may not answer that question in this book, but you sure will learn how I found that Warren Buffett uses Clean Surplus Accounting. And you will also find out how I, in my dissertation research work, took Clean Surplus Accounting and Buffett's work *ONE STEP BEYOND*.

Chapter 1

The Purpose of This Book—Your Journey

The purpose of this book is simple. It is written so that you, dear reader, can very easily develop your own set of portfolios, which should outperform most of the professional money managers of the world. It is written with the K.I.S.S. principle in mind: Keep It Simple, Silly!

Since the last publication of this book, we have proven that our growth strategy works as well as the doctoral research said it should. Our model portfolio has outperformed the S&P 500 Index by more than two to one over a 12-year compounded rate of return. Our model portfolio has also outperformed Buffett's Berkshire Hathaway by almost two to one over this same time period. This outstanding performance was achieved without taking on more than market risk. And now, we show you how to hedge (insure) those portfolios in order to lower risk to a very manageable level.

During the interim between the first edition and this book, we've developed a dividend growth and income portfolio, which uses the Clean

Surplus method as the basis for our stock selection. We want to select stocks with a 7 percent expected growth in dividends and another 8 percent anticipated growth in stock appreciation. This is a great portfolio, which all of us should have going into the future. We will show you how to structure your own dividend and income portfolio in Chapter 21.

We have added Chapter 25, which will discuss insuring our portfolios. Portfolio insurance costs money, but we will discuss how to generate extra money in our portfolios (enhanced income) in order to pay for that insurance.

The basis for our stock selection in both portfolios is our new computer program. Talk about making life easier in a manner that saves us hundreds and even thousands of hours. When I began my research, I had several classes of finance students who helped me with the original research. But they all eventually graduated, and I began to spend less time teaching and more time developing intellectual property. The answer, of course, was to find someone who could write a computer program that followed our proprietary algorithms. We will go over the use of the computer program we developed so that those who use it can structure their own portfolios. We've always had a computer program, but in the past several years we had a professional put his extensive touch on it, so even I can use it with great ease.

Finally, for folks who do not want to develop and monitor their portfolios themselves, we can direct you to professionals who are certified to use the Buffett and Beyond stock selection method to develop portfolios. This is one reason we developed our website, appropriately addressed as www.BuffettAndBeyond.com.

Please allow me some time to tell you what this book is not. This book is certainly not an accounting book. However, it does discuss Clean Surplus Accounting, which is very possibly the simplest accounting method based upon the easiest-to-understand principle in the world. It will be very easy for you to understand because you actually use it every day and so does someone who is admired by the entire investing world.

We will find out how Warren E. Buffett, the world's greatest investor, utilizes this method. We will learn that a very simple ratio developed from this method (which you also use all the time) will tell us almost all we need to know about a company's operating efficiency. We will then use this ratio to compare one company's operating efficiency with another company's operating efficiency. Following operating efficiency, the discussion will focus in great depth on why the most widely used ratio of comparison, return on equity (ROE), is so misused and misunderstood. Next, we will discuss why investors who use the traditional accounting ROE are doomed to underperform the averages.

The traditional accounting ROE *cannot* be used as a comparison ratio between companies. However, the ROE as configured by Clean Surplus is another story. In fact, it is our story.

Our next step will be to venture *one step beyond* and discuss my in-depth research on portfolio construction and how we can attempt to predict the future returns of our newly developed portfolios.

In other words, we will discover not only how to structure a superior performing portfolio, but we will also learn how to determine the predictability (or not) of the future total returns of that portfolio.

We will finally develop two very simple buy-and-hold portfolios. A buy-and-hold portfolio helps keep the taxman from becoming a partner in our everyday decisions, because it does not require everyday trading decisions. However, there are definitely rules on when to sell some of our portfolio positions.

I will always remember what a well-seasoned money manager told me just as I was beginning my education in the stock market. He wisely said that most times it was much better taking your client out to lunch rather than sitting in front of a computer screen trying to make those few extra dollars.

What he was trying to tell me was forget about short-term gains and concentrate on developing great long-term investment portfolios for the clients. Then you can spend all the extra time telling the clients about the merits of the superior portfolios you built for them instead of trying to trade those portfolios.

Thirty years later, this lesson helped me remember that I cannot single-handedly balance the U.S. budget deficit by paying extra taxes on those short-term gains that, to tell the truth, elude me to this day.

Warren Buffett has also formulated some pretty sound investment principles over the years. Let's learn from "the great one" and try not to reinvent the investing wheel. The man doesn't hide his thoughts or actions from us. It would be a foolhardy person who ignores Buffett's proven method of success.

SUMMARY

1. This book will show you a very simple system designed to exhibit the predictability (or not) of a company's operating performance.
2. We will learn how to structure a superior growth portfolio.
3. We will learn how to structure a superior dividend and growth portfolio.
4. You will learn how Warren Buffett, known as the world's greatest investor, uses this very simple system.
5. We will then discuss the research, which shows how to use the predictability of the simple accounting system called Clean Surplus in order to obtain superior portfolio performance.
6. We will later discuss some of the aspects of a company that Buffett looks for, which have earned his proven and successful results.

Chapter 2

About Warren Buffett

I'm not here to tell you all about the investing life of Warren Buffett. What I will discuss with you is how he uses just a few numbers from the income statement, at least to an extent that we can understand and utilize, in a very simplified manner. Thus, this book will not go into detail about Mr. Buffett. There are so many wonderful books already written about him, and every one of them I read in the past is certainly worth reading more than once. He has been called the "world's greatest investor" and the "greatest investor of this century." Whatever we call him, I know this for certain: We all want to be like Warren.

A friend of mine who is an admirer of Buffett (like really, who isn't?) once told me that just before he (my friend) died, he hoped Buffett's life (and not his own) would flash in front of him.

We were sitting at a beachside tiki hut in Florida, drinking one or four beers, when he mentioned flashing lives, so I wasn't sure if he was talking about Warren Buffett or Jimmy Buffett, but hey, we were happy talking about stocks (like Warren) and watching the ocean (like Jimmy). After all, isn't that the way it's supposed to be?

> If *used properly*, the numbers tell us almost everything we need to know about a company.

Now that we've discussed Warren Buffett's life in such great detail (I'm joking of course), let's talk about numbers. After all, I certainly believe that the numbers tell us almost everything we need to know about a company. Let me clarify this statement. If *used properly*, the numbers will tell us almost everything we need to know about a company.

If we use the correct numbers in the correct way, the bottom-line results will tell us which companies we want in our portfolio and which companies should be in someone else's portfolio. The problem is most analysts out there in "Investment Land" are using the wrong numbers. But after you finish with this book, we really won't care about the analysts out there in Investment Land.

Where is the Investment Land of which I speak? Top of the tower of Big Ben at midnight. Second star to the right and fly away 'til morning. Yes folks, many analysts and portfolio managers really believe that Never Never Land is the same place as Investment Land.

> Most investment analysts use the wrong numbers for stock selection. I know; I've taught many of the present and future analysts in my college classes.

How do I know most investors are using the wrong numbers for stock selection? I'm a college and university teacher (my third career). I teach my students finance the way (well, almost the way) the academic community demands finance be taught. My students then go out into the real world and use these very methods taught to them by the academic community. Most of the academic community truly believes that if you know accounting and finance, then you know how to select stocks for a portfolio.

Folks, this just isn't necessarily so, and I'll teach you why very soon. Let's just say this for now. As long as students are taught finance by the present establishment and then go out and use this knowledge in the investing community, Warren Buffett will always have job security as the world's greatest investor. Even in Never Never Land.

> Learning about finance and learning about investments are two totally different subjects. The problem is that most investment analysts don't understand this.

How do I know that the stock valuation models taught in colleges and universities don't work very well? If they did, all the college professors would be as rich as Warren Buffett. And guess what? They're not. They (the academics) think Buffett is just plain lucky. Oh believe me, the academic community has all the answers to the "luck" syndrome, but the bottom line is even though Buffett (and some others) have great track records, it doesn't matter to the academic community. Students just aren't taught the methods that produce the extraordinary results, because in the academic community "extraordinary" is considered luck, and luck cannot be predicted or tested through statistical analysis. But always remember what I say about luck. It is when opportunity meets preparation.

I've alluded to the fact that Warren Buffett uses Clean Surplus. How do I know this? Please remember that I wrote and published a several-hundred-page research paper (my dissertation) on the predictability of Clean Surplus. Please trust me that I know what Clean Surplus looks like when I see it.

One of the courses I taught at a nearby university was entitled Advanced Managerial Finance. The first case we analyzed each semester was "Warren E. Buffett, 1995." Yes, and on page 15, Exhibit No. 5, is a chart on a company named Scott & Fetzer, which was a company purchased by our idol, Warren Buffett. The chart came from the Berkshire Hathaway, Inc. Annual Report, 1994, p. 7. And yes, the chart was a chart using Clean Surplus Accounting. But it was very strange because the author of the text did not mention anything about Clean Surplus. In fact, the chart was just sitting there alone with nothing much said about it: just another exhibit in a case study designed to confuse the student.

Ah, but my students were not confused because they knew what Clean Surplus Accounting looked like, and when I pointed out the relationship between the chart and Clean Surplus, they quickly recognized the great importance of Exhibit No. 5 on page 15. My students understood what Warren Buffet saw in Scott & Fetzer, and it is what you will see in many stocks once you finish this book.

> Clean Surplus Accounting is not taught in our fine business schools. This is why Warren Buffett has job security.

The second and even more important instance of Warren Buffett using Clean Surplus Accounting can be found in the book *Buffettology* by Mary Buffett and David Clark. Mary is Warren's former daughter-in-law, and I would imagine she knows something about her father-in-law. Right there on page 124 in her workbook (which augments her first edition) is a chart (spreadsheet) of Coca-Cola. I know you know what the chart was. Yes, it was a chart showing owners' equity configured through the use of Clean Surplus Accounting.

Neither Mary nor David mention the term Clean Surplus Accounting. Not a mention of Clean Surplus Accounting is made in either *Buffettology* or the text I used in my advanced finance course. However, *Buffettology* begins to discuss predictability and Warren's use of this predictability. In no other book I've read on Warren Buffett will you see the mention of predictability. Dear reader, you will certainly see a lot of it in this book. So read on.

By the way, *Buffettology* is very good. Many of the books written about Warren Buffett do not cover the numbers extensively, because Buffett's life is so very interesting that the authors just do not have time for numbers. If you want to learn how to invest like Warren, you need to read books written by analysts and folks who know numbers. This book is one of those books. I know I would rather learn why a certain stock should be in my portfolio than whether Buffett did or did not have a headache on such and such a day back in 1960. Yes, this book teaches you how to invest, while most other books on Buffett's life do not.

In summary, you will not learn a great deal about Warren Buffett's life in the following pages. However, you will learn how Warren Buffett uses Clean Surplus Accounting and, more importantly, why he chooses to do so. After that, we will discuss my research and see if Clean Surplus Accounting can truly be used for predictability. I don't want to make you crazy and let you guess, so I'll tell you right now.

My work shows that, yes indeed, Clean Surplus Accounting measures predictability just as was suggested by the very fragmented literature that spans almost a century.

After the research, you will see how the research played out in model portfolios for more than a decade. What is so good about a second edition is you will be able to analyze a model portfolio over the past 12 years and see if it *really works*. And folks, it really does work. After all, the Clean Surplus method allows you to see which stocks are making the most money on money invested in a company. And if they've done well in the past at making shareholders wealthy, then the probability is that they will continue to do so into the future.

You see, we all know Warren Buffett is doing something right and after you read this book, you will know just exactly *what* he is doing right. And what he is doing right is called by us mere mortals "proven success."

SUMMARY

1. If *used properly*, the numbers tell us almost everything we need to know about a company.
2. Most investment analysts use the wrong numbers for stock selection. I know; I've taught many of the future analysts while teaching at several universities.
3. Learning about finance and learning about investments are two different subjects. The problem is that most investment analysts don't know this.
4. Clean Surplus Accounting is not taught in our fine business schools. This is why Warren Buffett has job security.
5. In future chapters, you will see the academic research, and then you will see more than a decade of results.

Chapter 3

Determining the Earning Capacity of a Company (Now Really, Can It Be This Easy?)

Value Is Determined by the Creation of Wealth

The most important concept in investing is to determine which companies are most efficient at using their asset base to earn profits for us, the shareholders. Earning profits should not be a short-term fad. Profits should be examined as to the level of the return on assets and the consistency of those returns. In other words, an efficient company can earn more with a certain asset base than the competition, and the most efficient company can do so consistently year after year after year.

> Profits should be examined as to the level of return on assets and the consistency of those returns.

Remember that little lemonade stand you set up in front of your house? Then one day your competition set one up right across the street. Somehow, you had to come up with a method in order to be more efficient than the competition. After all, if you were more efficient, you could price your product lower than the competition and still generate the same or greater profit.

Possibly you had a better and more efficient lemon squeezer (like mom), which would net you more juice per lemon. Maybe you had a competitive advantage in that you were set up under the only shady maple tree on the street. People wanted to stop at your stand because it was 100 degrees in the sun and you had the monopoly on shade. Maybe you allowed your workers (little brother and sister) to share in the profits of your lemonade stand. Always remember: *Ownership is a very powerful incentive.*

Get the picture? Sure you do. But how in the world do you look at two similar companies such as Pepsi and Coke and determine which company has the most efficient lemon squeezer or which company is operating under a shade tree during the summer? Going even further, how in the world can you compare two totally different companies in totally different industries such as Netflix and General Mills? Most analysts will tell you to pick a company in each industry so you will be very diversified in your holdings. I can tell you right here and now that there are some industries you just should not be part of. Not if you want to make money, that is.

The Beach Factor

Before we go on, I want you to be aware that I firmly believe in the "Beach Factor." The Beach Factor means that you can perform your work so efficiently that you have time to go to the beach. The Beach Factor is, of course, synonymous with free time. I recently bought a beautiful hammock, which is set up under that shade tree where the old lemonade stand stood so very many years ago. The hammock keeps calling my name so softly, "Come here and rest. Come here and take your mind off the world."

> The Beach Factor, of course, is synonymous with free time. If you are efficient in your work, you will eventually have lots of free time.

See? That's the Beach Factor. So keep in mind as we proceed through this book that we are fine-tuning your stock selection skills so that you, too, will have time to go to the beach. By the time you finish this book and become familiar with our computer program, you too will have the Beach Factor concept embedded in your life forever.

What's does that mean? Invest like Warren Buffett and live like Jimmy Buffett? Yes, that's the place we want to get to.

> If you want to live at the beach like Jimmy Buffett, you've got to learn how to invest like Warren Buffett.

As you can see throughout this book, I usually succeed in bringing concepts and examples down to my level of thinking, which is somewhere between daydreaming at the beach and the real world. I lean more toward the former than the latter because it's much more fun. The reason I say this is I don't want you daydreaming as I go through some very simple concepts because the very simple concepts are all part of the larger picture.

Clean Surplus

Clean Surplus is a very simple type of accounting. But please don't allow yourself to be turned off by the word "accounting." I know it brings back bad memories for some of you. Remember Accounting 101? I know, I know: not if you don't have to. And those of you who never had an accounting course, please don't worry. What we are about to discuss is hardly what you would associate with serious accounting. Trust me on this one; this is going to be easier than reading a good sea story.

I'm going to introduce you to Clean Surplus toward the end of this chapter. But it will be so very subtle that you won't even know you've been exposed to it. You will learn this concept and not even realize it until I jump up and tell you. Just remember that I really do believe in the K.I.S.S. principle.

Determining an Efficient Company

Question: What is an efficiently operated company?

Answer: It is a company that earns a very high return on the money invested into it (Clean Surplus owners' equity), and does so consistently year after year.

> An efficiently operated company is one that earns a *high* and *consistent* return on its asset base.

Before I go on, I want you all to understand that we use "book value," "asset base," and "owners' equity" to mean the same thing, at least for now. They really are not the same, but for now, just let it be.

Take Your Bank Account

Think of your bank account. Bank A consistently pays you 10 percent interest on your money year after year. Bank B pays you 10 percent one year, 8 percent the next year, 5 percent the following year, and 10 percent the year after that (Table 3.1).

Bank A is considered efficient because it earns a *high* and *consistent* rate of return on our invested money year in and year out. Bank B is not only relatively inconsistent in its returns, but is less efficient in the use of its assets because, overall, Bank B returns less on our invested money than does Bank A.

You see, investors like a high rate of return, and even more than a high rate of return, investors want a consistent rate of return. After all, this is why people invest in bonds.

Table 3.1   Which Bank Is Efficient?

Year	Bank A	Bank B
4	10%	10%
3	10%	5%
2	10%	8%
1	10%	10%

In order to go on with this book you must answer the following question correctly. The question is into which bank would you entrust your hard-earned money? Hey, correct! You've earned the right to continue. See? I told you this would be easy.

Just jumping ahead a bit, the analysis of the bank example is exactly how we're going to analyze stocks. Don't believe me? Read on.

Bonds

Sorry for the digression away from stocks, but think about bonds for a moment. People buy bonds for steady income. People buy bonds for a (relatively) high rate of return compared to other relatively low-risk investments such as bank accounts and CDs. However, some people want a higher return over the long term, which is why somebody invented the stock market. But if you want to win in the stock market (or successfully analyze a company), you want stocks that generate both a *high* and *consistent* return on the equity (money) that investors have put into the company.

You would like your stocks to act like a bond except you want *increasing* earnings year after year. If the increase in earnings is not consistent, then you are increasing the risk of ownership. The big question is: Why would you want to do that?

Earning Capacity

The earning capacity of a company (how much in earnings it makes) is a direct function of the size of its asset base and how efficiently that company utilizes that asset base. Let's begin with the size of the asset base.

Take two bank accounts, each with the same amount of risk, but paying us a different rate of interest. The account with Bank A contains $8,000 while the account with Bank B contains $10,000. We would naturally assume that the account held with Bank B would earn more interest for us as it is working with a larger asset base. However, Bank A is paying out a higher rate of interest to us because it is investing our deposits more efficiently. Thus, it is able to pay us a greater return.

Bank A $8,000 × **10%** = $800 in interest (earnings)
Bank B $10,000 × **5%** = $500 in interest (earnings)

> Bank account B has a larger asset base than Bank account A. But not only must we know the *size* of the asset base, we must also know the *rate of return* generated on that asset base in order to determine which bank is the most *efficient* bank.

Bank account B has a higher asset base and should earn a greater return for us, but it isn't because it is not making efficient use of money held in deposits. We see that bank A earns a greater *return* of $800 on a smaller asset base while Bank B is earning $500 for us on a larger asset base. A closer look reveals that Bank A is earning 10 percent on our invested equity while Bank B is earning just a 5 percent return on equity for us. Even though Bank B has a larger asset base, it is earning fewer dollars for us. Why? Because Bank B is earning a lower *percentage return* on its asset base than Bank A when it invests our deposited money. It is the ability to measure this *percentage return* that will mean so much in our analysis as we go on.

If both banks had the same amount in the accounts, Bank B would earn a much *lower* dollar amount than Bank A as shown next.

Bank A $10,000 × **10%** = $1,000 in interest (earnings)
Bank B $10,000 × **5%** = $500 in interest (earnings)

> We must know the *rate of return* (percentage return) on an asset base in order to know which is the more *efficient* bank.

The problem we are faced with in security analysis, which will be solved in this book, is how to determine the asset base of large companies and how to determine the percentage return on that asset base. And it's not the way finance people have been taught in the past. It is the method you will learn in this book that separates the great money managers from all the rest.

How to Determine the Operating Efficiency of a Company

Let's look at two separate bank accounts again as shown in Table 3.2, each with the same initial amount of $100 in each of them. Let's also assume all interest payments (earnings) are reinvested back into the account. Begin in year one at the bottom of each column and work your way up to year five. The percentages represent return on equity, or ROE.

Bank A begins year one with **$100**. Interest of **$10** was earned during year 1 and the entire $10 was reinvested (retained) back into the account. Thus, the following year (year two) begins with the original $100 plus the interest earned of $10 for a total of **$110**. Year two begins with an account size of $110.

As you can see, our asset base is growing as time goes on. As our asset base grows (because of reinvestment), we would expect to earn even more interest in year two. In year two, Bank A earns **$11** in interest for us. Then as the asset base grows each year (because we are *retaining* everything we earn), we generate a higher and higher amount of interest. Again, the higher amount of interest is due to the increasing size of the asset base.

Table 3.2   Bank A and Bank B—Initial Amount of $100

	Bank A			Bank B		
Year	Equity	Interest	ROE	Equity	Interest	ROE
5	$146.00	$14.60	10.00%	$142.45	$11.40	8.00%
4	$133.00	$13.30	10.00%	$131.29	$11.00	8.50%
3	$121.00	$12.10	10.00%	$120.45	$10.85	9.00%
2	$110.00	$11.00	10.00%	$110.00	$10.45	9.50%
1	$100.00	$10.00	10.00%	$100.00	$10.00	10.00%

Ah, but there's another very important part of this story. In fact, it is the most important part. The very serious question is what percentage return are we earning on our equity, and even more important, is it a consistent return year after year?

To find the answer to this very important question, we simply divide what we made in interest (earnings) for any particular year by the amount of money (equity) with which we began the year.

Looking at Bank A for the first year, we see that we earned $10 on the $100 in the account at the beginning of the year. In order to determine the ROE simply take the $10 earned and divide it by the amount of money ($100) with which we began the year (Table 3.3).

So simply, $10/$100 = 10 percent. This is ROE.

Bank B began year one with the same amount of $100. We earned $10 that year, which gave us a 10 percent ROE, which is the same as Bank A.

In year two, we began the year (in both accounts) with $110. Bank A returned $11, but Bank B returned just $10.45. Bank A's ROE was 10 percent once again, but Bank B returned $10.45/$110 for just a 9.5 percent ROE.

Let's jump ahead and look at year five for both bank accounts. Bank A began the year with $146 in equity. It earned interest (earnings) of $14.60 for us that year. We made $14.60 on an asset base of $146 for an ROE of 10 percent ($14.60/$146). This is a very good scenario because we want a high and consistent rate of return from our investments, and Bank A is providing a relatively *high* and *consistent* rate of return for us.

Bank B began year five with $142.45 in equity. It earned interest (earnings) of $11.40. $11.40 divided by $142.45 is an 8 percent ROE. We see that Bank B is not providing us with a high and consistent ROE when compared to Bank A.

Let's take these results and put them into real terms used in the investing world. In year five, Bank A had a 10 percent ROE while Bank B had an 8 percent ROE.

Table 3.3   Bank A in First Year

Year	Equity	Interest	ROE
1	$100.00	$10.00	10.00%

The earning capacity of a company (how much in earnings it makes) is a direct function of 1) the size of its asset base and 2) how efficiently that company utilizes that asset base.

Sooo Important

Dear reader, the previous example is so very important because it is the very basic fiber of investing. If you can answer the following questions, you are well on your way to being able to develop your own, above-average performing portfolio. This means that you will outperform 96 percent of the professional money managers over any average 10-year period.

Question #1
Why does Bank Account A have more money in it (equity) in year five when both accounts began with $100 in year one?

Answer
Because Bank A earned a *higher* and more *consistent* rate of return. Bank A had a higher ROE than did Bank B.

Question #2
Why did Bank A earn a higher ROE than Bank B?

Answer
Who cares? Ok, you may think I'm being silly here, but really, who cares? Think about banks in real life. One is paying you 4 percent on your savings and another is paying 5 percent. Really now, when was the last time you sat down and asked how the banks were investing their (your) money? As my students would say, like, er, uh, like never!

You See . . . ROE Tells Us Everything

Hey, wait a minute! Is the example with Bank A and Bank B simple? Of course it is. And do you know what I just did? I just taught you Clean Surplus Accounting. Hellooo! Did you hear me? *You just learned Clean Surplus Accounting!!!*

And the name is exactly what it means. It's nice and *clean.* And the *surplus,* in its simplest terms, is the profit. And from Clean Surplus, which is how we figured the equity in the bank year after year, we were able to calculate the ROE generated by both banks. And because we were able to calculate the ROE *in the same manner* for each bank, we were able to determine the most efficient bank. Even more importantly, we now know which bank we should be putting our hard-earned money into.

You see, the ROE that we just configured using, yes, say it again, Clean Surplus Accounting, tells us almost everything we need to know about a bank or a company. If the ROE is *high* and *consistent* over the years relative to other banks or companies, we know which of these banks or companies we should be considering for investment of our hard-earned dollars.

Let's Ask Warren

Let's for a moment go from banks to companies and ask what Warren Buffett would begin to look for in a company.

First of all, he would say he wants a company with a *high* ROE and a *consistent* ROE. How do we know he says this? In Robert Bruner's *Case Studies in Finance,* he (Bruner) tells us that "Buffett sought to judge the simplicity of the business, the consistency of its operating history, the attractiveness of its long-term prospects, the quality of management, and the firm's capacity to create value."

Wow, all that? Gee, Professor, how can I determine all of this? I'm certainly no Warren Buffett!

Well, let's analyze what Buffett said and take this step-by-step and relate these qualities to the ROE from Clean Surplus Accounting. You know, Clean Surplus is the ROE we just figured using our bank examples.

1. If the ROE is *high* and *consistent*, we can pretty much assume the company has a good quality of management. A *high* and *consistent* ROE means management is doing things the right way.
2. If the ROE is *high* and *consistent*, we know the firm has the capacity to create value because it is already doing so.
3. If the ROE is *high* and *consistent* and the past is any indication of the future, we can assume the firm will have attractive long-term prospects.

Hey, what about the simplicity of the business? Buffett says he understands ice cream better than he understands computer software. And Buffett is smart. I'm sure he understands computer software.

Yes, but here's the real story. Buffett understands where the ice cream business will be in 10 years, but he has a hard time trying to figure out what the computer business will be like in 10 years or how the present companies in the computer business will be positioned in the whole scheme of things in 10 years.

So if you take a business that you understand and that company has a *high* and relatively *consistent* ROE, you are probably looking at a pretty good contender for your stock portfolio. You will learn more about *high* and *consistent* as we go along. After all, selecting stocks for our portfolio is what this book is all about.

Summary—the Key to the Investing Business

The key to investing is really very simple. We want to invest in companies that have a relatively *high* ROE, and we want companies that have a very *consistent* ROE.

Didn't you figure out very quickly into which bank you wanted to invest your hard-earned money? Selecting stocks for your portfolio is almost this easy. I'll prove to you later on (yes, another sea story) that even a blind person can select good stocks using exactly what you've learned so far. Yes, I said a blind person.

Why Hasn't the Entire World Figured This Out Yet?

Wait a minute, Professor; this chapter was pretty simple. I hear about ROE all the time. Everybody uses ROE. What's up here?

Well, my dear readers, the entire world has gone in a different direction relative to the calculation of ROE. The entire world uses the traditional accounting ROE and *not* the Clean Surplus ROE, and this difference in calculating the ROE makes *all* the difference in the world.

It is the difference between structuring an average portfolio and constructing a superior performing portfolio. It is the difference between buying the S&P 500 Index (in one form or another) or developing a very simple, above-average-performing portfolio and going to the beach. Please remember the Beach Factor.

You Will Learn

Between what you will learn from Mr. Buffett and the results you will observe from my research, your investment philosophy will be changed forever. And it will be changed for the better. As I say to both you and my students, this stuff is a piece of cake!

SUMMARY

1. Buffett uses numbers in a different manner than most people.
2. Buffett is cool. Buffett is more successful than most others, and we want to find out why.
3. If *used properly*, the numbers tell us almost everything we need to know about a company.
4. The earning capacity of a company (how much in earnings it makes) is a direct function of the size of its asset base and how efficiently that company utilizes that asset base.
5. Most investment analysts use the wrong numbers in their stock selection process. I know; I've taught many of our future analysts in college.
6. Learning about finance and learning about investments are two different subjects. The problem is that most investment analysts don't know this.
7. Clean Surplus Accounting is not taught in our fine business schools. This is why Warren Buffett has job security.
8. Buffett wants to invest in companies that he understands. And he needs to understand the business environment and where a company will be in that business environment 10 years from now. The future of ice cream is easier to determine than the future of computer software companies.

9. Companies we choose for our portfolios must be efficient. They must have a *high* and *consistent* ROE as configured by Clean Surplus Accounting.
10. Clean Surplus Accounting is a piece of cake. Clean Surplus Accounting is so easy, you just learned it in this chapter and didn't even know you learned it.

Chapter 4

My Theory of Why Most Money Managers of the World Cannot Outperform the Market Averages

I would like to take a time out from numbers for a little bit while we let the last chapter sink in. Let's take this occasion to discuss the academic world that spawns the future accountants and finance professionals (analysts and money managers) of the world.

If you look at the statistics of money manager returns you will see headlines in any given year such as, "75 percent of the money managers (of publicly traded stock mutual funds) UNDERPERFORMED the market averages over the past year."

One study showed that out of the 25 percent of the money managers who were able to outperform the market in any given year, 67 percent of those money managers did not outperform the averages the following year. Of course, by market averages we are speaking of the Dow Jones 30 Industrials and/or the S&P 500 Index.

Over the longer term, fewer and fewer money managers are able to outperform the averages over the entire time period. I recently read that over any 10-year period, just 4 percent of the money managers are able to outperform the S&P 500 Index on a risk-adjusted basis. Please remember when we speak of outperforming or not outperforming the averages, we are speaking about portfolios, which exhibit the *same risk* or have the returns adjusted for the same risk as the Dow or the S&P 500.

> The efficient market hypothesis basically says that no one can consistently outperform the market averages.

The aforementioned performance statistics lend credibility to the followers of the efficient market hypothesis (EMH). Real world performance gives the academics a lot of ammunition, as the efficient market hypothesis is a mainstay of academic research. The academics look at the returns of the publicly traded common stock mutual funds and right there in black and white are the multitudes of mutual fund money managers who cannot outperform the Dow or the S&P 500 averages.

I subscribe, from time to time, to the Morningstar database. Morningstar is the publication that follows and rates mutual funds, just as Value Line is best known for its analysis of individual stocks.

I "asked" the Morningstar database which mutual funds were outperforming the S&P 500 Index over any 1-, 3-, or 10-year period. One thing I noticed was that the funds that were underperforming the S&P 500 were doing so on average by about 1.5 percent per year. Well, it just so happens that this amount turns out to be the cost associated with running most publicly traded mutual funds. My observation told me that most money managers are able to perform almost as well as the index averages, but the return to the shareholder was less due to operating expenses.

Please be aware that any time you look at a database such as Morningstar, the results will almost always be different depending on the particular day you are searching the database. If you look at the database today, the three-year results will be different from the three-year results if you perform your tests tomorrow. In other words, this is not pure research. It is merely an observation.

> Students, the future analysts and future money managers of our country, are driven crazy by the academic world. They are taught that they cannot outperform the market averages.

Bruner, in *Case Studies in Finance*, quotes Andrew Kilpatrick in *Of Permanent Value*, p. 353, who in turn quotes Buffett in that "It has been helpful to me [Buffett] to have tens of thousands turned out of business schools taught that it didn't do any good to think."

First of all, this is scary, but why do you think Buffett says this? I'll tell you why right now. Remember that I began a teaching career *after* I spent 22 years seriously investing in real estate and the stock market. Thus, I was exposed to all the theory *after* I learned how to survive in the real world. What a shocker to be exposed to the academic teachings *after* you've already learned the survival skills needed to be fairly successful.

Once I had my doctoral degree in hand and was able to teach full-time at the college and university level, I sometimes taught the Principles of Finance course in which I taught students the efficient market hypothesis. This theory tells us that you cannot use past information, present information, or inside information in order to outperform the market averages. Actually, the meaning of this theory is that all information is already reflected in the price of a stock and, thus, you cannot use any information to gain *abnormal returns* on your chosen stocks.

Of course, I always wondered what "abnormal" meant. Abnormal is anything that is not normal. But it is at the discretion of the writer to tell us what normal is so that we can understand what he or she means by abnormal in any given circumstance.

> Efficient market theory: All information about a company is always fully reflected in the price of its stock.

You may think I'm being a bit foolish here, but let me give you an example. Let's talk about earnings. You may read an academic headline shouting out that Company X generated abnormal returns (earnings) for a certain period. Again, only academics would say such a thing. Abnormal could mean that 6 percent is normal because 6 percent might be the present cost of cash at that particular time. In other words, you could earn a 6 percent return on a T-Bond at that particular time.

Or normal could be the amount of earnings the "average" company in the S&P 500 earned during a particular time frame. Thus, abnormal returns would be above (or below) the average earnings returns for the S&P 500 stocks. Or abnormal could be the earnings returns above the normal (average) earnings returns of that particular stock over a particular period of time.

Confused? The lesson here is don't read academic articles unless forced under duress of death.

Back to the students of the world: In the Principles of Finance course, students are taught that under the efficient market hypothesis, they cannot outperform the markets because there are no mispriced securities. In other words, all securities are fairly priced because their price reflects all available and nonavailable information about those securities at any particular time.

Some people have taken literary license in deciphering the meaning of the hypothesis. You've heard stories such as a stock picker who cannot select a portfolio that will outperform one picked by a person who randomly selects stocks from the *Wall Street Journal*.

Random selection has taken on a less serious meaning in the past 15 years or so. Now, they (whoever is being most ridiculous at the time) will have a monkey select a portfolio of stocks. Not long after the monkey, the random stock picker will become a blindfolded monkey throwing darts at pages of the *Wall Street Journal*.

My Contest—Beware How You Select the Random Portfolio

Just to add to the fun, I once ran my very own stock-picking contest. I contacted over 60 students in the doctoral program at Nova Southeastern University and had them select a portfolio of up to 10 stocks that would be held for one year without change. Four of these people were professionals in the world of money management.

I then very scientifically selected a market portfolio against which the contestants would compete. My scientific method was to have my wife cover her eyes and point to stocks in the *Wall Street Journal*. Thus, her selection became the randomly selected portfolio. Much to my dismay, my wife eventually heard about the blindfolded monkey and, of course, she thought she was the . . . er . . . well, you get the picture. It took many long-stemmed roses for me to even get back into the house, let alone back on speaking terms.

The contest? Oh yes, the contest. The professional money managers were in the bottom half of all contestants. The randomly selected portfolio was also in the bottom half. But the portfolio selected by the Clean Surplus method came in third. The portfolios that came in first and second consisted of just one security each. These guys went for broke in order to win the contest. The portfolio that earned last place also consisted of just one security.

Hey, not very scientific, you say? Of course not, but we're talking about monkeys and professional stock pickers, so don't talk to me about scientific.

Back to My Students

After my students become brainwashed by academic theory telling them they cannot outperform the market averages, they then take an advanced course called (of course) Advanced Managerial Finance. This is a case study course, in which the students study cases of well-known companies. They get to see charts and balance sheets and income statements and cash flow statements and, and, ...

In all cases, something goes wrong and the company gets itself into trouble. The students must then use the financial statements to try and find out if the problems could have been foreseen.

One Step Beyond Buffett

Warren Buffett, more or less, says his job as the world's greatest investor is secure because the money managers of the world were once taught that it does no good to use either fundamental or technical analysis to select a superior performing security. The reason for this is that, according to the efficient market hypothesis, all the information about a stock—past, present and inside information—is already reflected in the price of that stock. The money managers try to outperform the averages, but in the black recesses of their minds there is a little voice whispering to them that they cannot outperform the averages. And you know what? Very few of them are able to outperform the averages.

But I take Buffett's analysis of the situation one step further. I use my vast knowledge of psychology (not!) to justify that the future money managers are just plain confused. You see, they are first taught it doesn't do any good to think (in the first finance course) and then they are taught they can look at the accounting numbers and discover that a company is about to get into trouble.

Taking this a bit further, if they can discover by using the accounting numbers that a company is getting into trouble, shouldn't they be able to look at the numbers and tell if a company is doing everything right and *not* getting itself into trouble? And if this is so, then shouldn't they be able to construct a portfolio of those "good" companies and leave out the "bad" companies and have this "good" portfolio outperform the averages? Don't forget: The market averages contain both the "good" and the "bad" companies.

So in the first finance class they are taught they cannot select good companies, and in the second class they are taught they certainly can select good companies through elimination of the "bad" companies. Is this enough to drive you crazy? Following this non-logical logic, it is my theory that all these students are driven crazy by the academic world. How can we expect our brightest to perform well if we drive them crazy while still in college?

You Don't Have to Worry

Now you know why you really don't have to worry about all those professional money managers outperforming your very own self-selected portfolio. First of all, they are suffering from the, "no you can't, yes you can" syndrome and second of all, they don't know about Clean Surplus Accounting. Why? Because Clean Surplus Accounting is not well known in the academic world and is not taught in our fine business schools. And furthermore, Clean Surplus Accounting is much too simple to be considered to have credence with the academic community.

So there you have it. Only you, me, and Warren Buffett know about Clean Surplus Accounting. And folks, we are all that matter.

Fun with Our Portfolio Reviews

The great thing about writing a second edition to a book after 11 years is you can fill in with another 11 years of research and findings. During this time frame, we ran a very successful radio program, which was more fun than a person should be allowed to have. It is also more work than a person should have to do, but while we were putting on the show five days a week, we analyzed more stocks (for the show) than there were stocks in the universe.

One thing we did on the show was to have folks e-mail us their portfolios so we could analyze their stocks relative to the Clean Surplus method. You will see further on in this book that the research and more than a decade of CPA-reviewed portfolios show (now think of the bank account example) that portfolios made up of stocks with higher (Clean Surplus) returns on equity (ROEs) outperform portfolios made up of stocks with lower ROEs.

OK, what is high and what is low? The *average* ROE of all the stocks in the S&P 500 index is about 14 percent. Fourteen percent is a very important dividing line as you will see in upcoming chapters, but for now let's just use 14 percent as our dividing line for this story.

The First Finding: The very first amazing thing that I discovered about the stocks contained in almost every one of the portfolios sent in to us was that folks selected portfolios of stocks in which half the stocks had Clean Surplus ROEs above 14 percent and half the stocks had Clean Surplus ROEs below 14 percent. I was extremely surprised by this finding, but when I thought about it, it was perfectly explainable.

I reasoned that when selecting stocks, we do so by guessing. We read about stocks and watch TV investing shows and that's how we get our tips and our tips turn into actual purchases. Well, if we are pretty much "guessing" at stocks that we "think" should be in our portfolios, it is only natural that half of the stocks chosen would be above a certain threshold (14 percent ROE) and half the stocks would be below that threshold.

The Second Finding: The second finding was very much in line with my research and also true-to-life portfolios. The stocks in the portfolios that had higher ROEs (more than 14 percent) outperformed the stocks in the portfolios that had ROEs of 14 percent and lower.

Please be aware that this is backward looking. I took all the stocks and researched their performance over the *previous* five years. Later in this book you will see the *following* three years, which is very impressive indeed. But for now, let's concentrate on the portfolios as I performed the data testing.

In most cases, had these folks just invested in the stocks with ROEs above 14 percent just five years prior and left out the stocks with 14 percent ROEs and lower, they would have on average, more than doubled their money over those previous five years.

In Summary

I think you are beginning to see that we don't have to find a blindfolded monkey to throw darts at the *Wall Street Journal*, and we don't have to "guess" which stocks to put in our portfolios. All we have to do is click a button on our computer program that you will have free access to for four weeks upon purchasing this book, select stocks with the highest ROEs and then go to the beach. Sure, there are a few rules to follow, but folks, with the help of our tools, selecting good portfolios is really very easy. Very, very easy. And very, very easy means you are learning to apply the Beach Factor.

SUMMARY

1. Most money managers cannot outperform the market averages. Those who do have less than a 33 percent chance of continuing this performance through the second year.

2. Clean Surplus Accounting is not taught in our fine business schools. Therefore, those who understand Clean Surplus Accounting have a distinct advantage over those who have not had access to this method of accounting, which includes just about all the college graduates of this country.

3. Most folks will select "average" portfolios. However, using our simple tools that calculate the Clean Surplus ROE, picking stocks that are above average is very, very easy.

4. Selecting a superior portfolio in a short amount of time is very efficient. Efficiency in portfolio selection means you will have more time for the beach.

Chapter 5

A Very Simple Income Statement and an Even Simpler Balance Sheet

T his chapter is for everyone including the novice investor, the finance professional, and the seasoned accountant. We will thoroughly discuss some common and yet very important terms, but we want to make sure you understand *how* they will be used in the following text. The finance people and accountants may use certain terms a bit differently than they are used in Clean Surplus Accounting. Thus, in order to fully understand the concept of Clean Surplus, we must all begin on the same page.

If you don't understand any part of the next several pages, don't worry. We will go over this information again and again as we go along.

The rest of this book will differentiate the average investor and the professional money manager from you, who, after understanding this book, will be able to outperform all those around you most of the time and certainly over the long term. Why? Because Clean Surplus allows you to find the companies making the most efficient use of investment capital.

Let's get on with some simple but very important concepts. Please be aware that I am taking great literary license in order to make these concepts as simple as possible.

The Income Statement

The income statement is also called the "statement of operations" or a "profit and loss" (P&L) statement. In other words, money in (revenues and/or sales) minus money out (expenses) leaves us with net income.

Income Statement

Revenues
minus expenses, interest, taxes
=Net Income
minus non-recurring items
=Earnings
Earnings *minus* **Dividends = Retained Earnings**

Continuing on, net income less certain non-recurring items, *which are unique to a single company and not part of ordinary, everyday operations,* leaves us with earnings.

Earnings minus dividends paid out to investors (shareholders) equals retained earnings. Retained earnings is the money put back (retained) into the company so the company can grow.

These are Clean Surplus Accounting terms and will be used in this manner for the remaining chapters of this book.

That's it for the income statement as far as we are concerned. This is all we will use from here on in.

The Balance Sheet

The balance sheet tells us how much the company is worth. Or at least that's what they tell us in school. Assets minus liabilities equals the amount that the company is supposedly worth. This value is termed "book value" or "owners' equity."

In other words, what the company *owns* (assets) minus what the company *borrowed* (liabilities) from the bank and/or bondholders equals the book value or owners' equity.

Balance Sheet

Assets

minus all liabilities

=**Book Value** *or* **Owners' Equity**

The term book value is used interchangeably with owners' equity. The problem is even though book value *numerically* equals owners' equity on the balance sheet, these terms are defined differently. And therein lies the really, really big problem.

1. Book value is defined as assets minus liabilities just as we showed earlier.
2. Owners' equity is defined as how much money the owners of the company (stockholders) have put into the company through the sale of common stock as well as all the profits that were put back into the company over the years. These retained profits are called "retained earnings."

This discrepancy in meaning between book value and owners' equity is what Clean Surplus Accounting is all about. The next several chapters are designed to clear up that difference.

Tying Together the Income Statement and Balance Sheet

If a company shows a profit on the income statement and reinvests this profit back into the company, then the company must be worth more, just as our bank account was worth more when we retained (reinvested) the interest we earned each year.

The profit that is shown on the income statement, minus any dividends paid to stockholders is the retained earnings. Retained earnings are the portion of earnings that are reinvested back into the company and, of course, retained earnings will increase the value of the company. This added value will be shown (must be shown) on the balance sheet (statement of net worth) because the company is worth more. Remember, the balance sheet shows the book value or owners' equity of the company. The book value and owners' equity is also known as the "net worth" of the company.

The Link Between the Income Statement and Balance Sheet

Figure 5.1 shows how the income statement and balance sheet tie together. Once again, the profit (earnings) from the income statement, minus money paid out to stockholders (dividends), equals the retained earnings or money reinvested back into the company for future growth. The extra earnings not paid out to investors as dividends (retained Earnings) are carried over to the balance sheet (arrow), which in turn, increases the book value or owners' equity of the company.

This makes sense (cents), because if the company earns a profit and that profit is kept inside the company, then the company must be worth more. Think of our bank account examples. If we left the interest earned in the account, the account increased in value.

The retained earnings add to the value of the company and this value is shown on the balance sheet as an increase in book value or owners' equity. This is why retained earnings is called the *link* or *tie-in* between the income statement and the balance sheet.

There you have it. This is really as complicated as it gets. Let's now get on with the reasoning behind the structuring of a superior performing portfolio and your education of separating the men and women from the boys and girls.

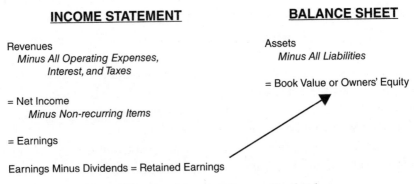

INCOME STATEMENT

Revenues
  Minus All Operating Expenses,
    Interest, and Taxes

= Net Income
  Minus Non-recurring Items

= Earnings

Earnings Minus Dividends = Retained Earnings

BALANCE SHEET

Assets
  Minus All Liabilities

= Book Value or Owners' Equity

Figure 5.1   Retained Earnings Carrying Over to Book Value

SUMMARY

1. There are two main statements in accounting that we are concerned with in Clean Surplus: the income statement and the balance sheet.

2. The income statement is also known as the profit and loss (P&L) statement and the statement of operations. This statement tells us how much the company is earning during a certain time period. Very simply put, money in and money out.

3. The balance sheet is also called the statement of net worth. It consists of all the assets a company owns minus everything the company owes out such as mortgages on property or loans from banks and investors.

4. The earnings number after dividends are paid out is called retained earnings. Retained earnings is the profit (or loss) from the income statement, which goes over to the balance sheet and adds (or subtracts) from net worth. If the company makes a profit and retains it within the company in order to grow (retained earnings), it will then add to net worth. If a company operates at a loss, the loss will subtract from net worth and the company is worth less.

Chapter 6

The Return on Equity Ratio

What is the difference between the traditional accounting return on equity (ROE) we hear about every day and the Clean Surplus Accounting ROE?

Answer: EVERYTHING!

Note: This is the most important chapter in the book. This chapter contains the knowledge that separates you from the rest of the world. Even if you don't understand as much as you'd like to at first, the rest of the book works with this information so that you will understand everything very soon. And for your diligent efforts, you will be rewarded for the rest of your life.

What you must remember for this chapter:
1. Book value is used interchangeably with equity (owners' equity), even though they do not have the same definition.

2. The ROE ratio is the most widely used (misused) method of comparing the operating efficiency of one company to the operating efficiency of another company.
3. In accounting, the *return* portion of ROE is earnings from the income statement, and the *equity* portion of ROE is book value (owners' equity) from the balance sheet.

What we will learn in this chapter:
1. The traditional accounting ROE is an extremely *inefficient method* of comparing the operating efficiency of one company to the operating efficiency of another company. This ROE is extremely inconsistent from year to year for most companies.
2. The Clean Surplus ROE is the *only reliable method* of comparing the operating efficiency of one company to the operating efficiency of another company. Clean Surplus smoothes out the ROE so that we can use it for analysis.

The ROE ratio is the most widely used ratio in all of Investment Land in order to compare the operating efficiency of a company to that of another company. However, there is a huge difference between the traditional accounting ROE as configured by the accounting numbers (which everyone uses) and the ROE as configured by Clean Surplus, which we use.

You already know the basics of Clean Surplus. It is your bank account. However, the traditional accounting ROE is different. The accounting ROE has three very major flaws:

1. The return part of the equation is not configured to conform to all companies.
2. The equity part of the equation is not configured to conform to all companies.
3. It just plain doesn't work as a comparison ratio.

The third and, of course, main flaw is that it just doesn't work. How do we know this? Because most of the money managers in Investment Land cannot outperform the averages. And since accounting ROE is the most widely used comparison ratio, then intuitively we know that the accounting ROE is not working relative to comparing the operating efficiency of one company relative to any other company.

We also know it doesn't work because in all my advanced finance classes I have my students run association (correlation) tests between the traditional accounting book value (equity) and stock returns. The association is very low. In fact, there is almost no association.

However, when the students run association tests between Clean Surplus book value (equity) and stock returns, the association is very high. This means that Clean Surplus book value (equity) has a direct correlation with the value (price) of a company, but accounting book value definitely does not.

Please remember that Warren Buffett says that (accounting) book value is meaningless relative to the intrinsic value of a company (Bruner, *Case Studies in Finance*). However, Buffett in his 2002 Annual Report to Shareholders speaks so fondly of book value. In fact, he talks about how well the book value of his investing company, Berkshire Hathaway, has grown.

How in the world can he say that book value is meaningless as an indicator of intrinsic value and then on the other hand talk about book value having great importance when he relates book value to his Berkshire Hathaway company? The answer could be that he may be talking about two different book values. Why don't we find out?

We will show the results of the association tests and predictability of Clean Surplus book value when we apply Clean Surplus book value to the ROE ratio in later chapters. We also show later that the Clean Surplus ROE has a very high relationship to the future returns of a stock portfolio. In other words, we see that, indeed, there is predictability in Clean Surplus Accounting and Clean Surplus ROE. And the desire for predictability is why Clean Surplus was invented.

This Chapter and the Next and the Next

In the following chapters we will cover the return portion and the equity portion of the ROE ratio. After that we will then show you how to determine a true Clean Surplus equity number.

We will see why the ROE from the accounting statements (traditional accounting ROE) *does not* represent a ratio that can be used to compare one company's operating efficiency to another company's operating efficiency. We will also learn why Clean Surplus Accounting ROE *does indeed* represent the best method of comparison of the operating efficiency of a company.

First, let's review just one thing. Earlier in this book, we calculated the earning capacity of a company (bank examples) by using the ROE as configured by Clean Surplus. It is simply the amount *earned* during a certain period divided by the amount of money with which we *began* that period.

We perform this calculation ourselves all the time for our own bank accounts and our own stock accounts. We are concerned not only with the dollar amount we earned during a particular period, but more importantly, the *percentage return* we earned during a particular period. All we need to know is how much we started with and how much we ended up with. Why do we use percentage returns? Because percentages are easily understood and thus easily compared to other companies.

Very simply, if we began with $100 and ended up with $112, we would want to brag about how much we made. We know we earned $12.

Next, we want to know what a profit of $12 represents in percentage terms. Simply put, the profit we earned ($12) divided by the amount we began with ($100) is 12 percent.

The formula is:

$$(\text{ending value} - \text{beginning value})/\text{beginning value}$$

The common term for this result in the world of investing is ROE or return on owners' equity.

> The ROE is the amount of money earned in a certain period divided by the amount of money at the beginning of that period.

The ROE in this example is Clean Surplus. If we could perform the same calculations for companies as we do for our bank account, we would be able to compare the ROE of one company to the ROE of another company because we are performing the calculations the exact same way for both companies. The companies with a higher and more consistent ROE would be the companies with which we would grace our portfolios. And this is what we will certainly discuss very thoroughly in the next several chapters.

However, before we go on, I want to make sure you understand or, for now, are at least aware that the ROE we calculate using Clean Surplus is not the traditional accounting ROE we see and hear about every day.

> The traditional accounting ROE that you hear about all the time is not the same as the Clean Surplus ROE that you are learning in this book.

You see, the people who use Clean Surplus ROE outperform the averages. Those who use the traditional accounting ROE (most everybody) fail, on the whole, to consistently outperform the averages. How can I say this? Both the academic research and actual life experience agree with this statement.

The next several chapters will show you how the traditional accounting ROE fails, but right now I will tell you *why* this ratio fails. It fails because the traditional accounting ROE is not a very good comparison ratio. In fact, it is just miserable as a comparison ratio, end of statement, but the beginning of a new investing career for you.

SUMMARY

1. A ratio commonly misused as a measure of comparability is the ROE ratio.
2. The traditional accounting ROE is not a good measure of comparability, as it wasn't meant to be a measure of comparability *between* different companies.
3. The Clean Surplus Accounting ROE was designed by the accounting profession to be a true measure of comparability between all companies. It was also designed to be a predictor of the future earnings of a company.
4. The Clean Surplus ROE allows us to determine which company is operating more efficiently in its use of the equity raised by the company from its investors.
5. The rest of this book will allow you to become an expert on the use of the Clean Surplus ROE as a measure of comparability and predictability.

Chapter 7

The Return Portion
of the Return on
Equity Ratio

The return number used in the traditional accounting return on equity (ROE) ratio is the earnings number from the income statement. *But the return number in clean surplus is not the earnings number.* The income statement (see the following section) shows money in, money out, and the amount left over.

The Income Statement: Return

Note: I understand the term "net income" may be used differently in the accounting profession than we are using it here. But to keep everyone on the same page, let's use it this way: Our net income is earnings before non-recurring items such as extraordinary items and future liabilities according to the American Institute of CPAs (AICPA) position.

I mentioned that the income statement shows money in and money out. Well, up to a point:

Income Statement
Revenues
minus all operating expenses including depreciation, interest, and taxes
=Net income

Here's what we have: Money in, which is *revenues* and/or *sales,* minus money out, which is all *recurring* operating *expenses* along with interest and taxes. The amount left over is called "net income."

By the way, net income is the return portion of Clean Surplus ROE, and is figured the same among all companies. However, net income is not the return portion of traditional accounting ROE. Please read on.

If this were all there was to it, we would use the net income as the return portion in the ROE ratio to compare one company to another because it is simply money in, money out, and thus, profit (net income). Net income is figured the same way for every company. *One point:* Depreciation is an expense. It is not money out, but depreciation is used as an expense to determine net income.

However, there are other items that must be taken into consideration for individual companies. These items are collectively termed "non-recurring" items and include such items as extraordinary losses (or gains) and future liabilities, and they are deducted (or added) *after* net income.

Income Statement
Revenues
minus all operating expenses including depreciation, interest, and taxes
=Net income
minus non-recurring items such as extraordinary losses (or gains)
=Earnings

The earnings represent the return portion of the traditional accounting ROE. However, because earnings are calculated *after* the non-recurring items, which are *unique to each individual company,* earnings should not ever, ever be used to compare one company's earnings to that of another company's earnings.

You can see by this income statement that something else has come into the picture. Just after the net income number, which *is* calculated the same way for all companies, we see non-recurring items, such as extraordinary losses and future liabilities, which are subtracted from net income to give us earnings. These unique non-recurring items are *not* the same for all companies and thus not comparable relative to the operations of a company.

Extraordinary losses (or gains) are extraordinary. In other words, they do not occur during the ordinary operations of the company. Here's the really important part. These items are *unique* to each individual company and thus, are not comparable.

Certainly, these unique events must be accounted for and they are. But in no way do these events show how efficiently you've been running your operation. And we're concerned with *operating efficiency* in our ROE ratio and not branches falling out of the sky because of a hurricane passing by.

Efficiency (or lack of) occurs every day. Unique items do not happen during ordinary operations and many may occur just once in a lifetime. The point is the earnings are very much affected by these unique events. They are not predictable and thus not comparable.

It is emphasized in Clean Surplus literature that the entries after net income *do not lend themselves to predictability*, because extraordinary events are not predictable.

> Clean Surplus Accounting tells us that the entries after net income *do not lend themselves to predictability*, because extraordinary events are not predictable.

Look at the other line under net income, labeled future liabilities. A future liability is a liability that will occur in the future and not today. In fact, there is no money outflow at the present time for this line item. A future liability may be future medical benefits for the workers who have not yet retired. This is a future liability, but it is not money flowing out of the company today. It is not an actual, present-day reduction in the *asset base* of the company.

In accounting, we are given the choice of subtracting some liabilities from net income either all at once or slowly over a period of years and different companies may select different time periods.

We will look at a huge future liability for General Motors in just a minute. In fact, General Motors experienced a whopping 80 percent reduction in total company value because of this one item. However, it only experienced an 80 percent reduction on paper and not on its real asset value. More on this very important event a bit later.

Bottom line: All you must remember here is that the items which are listed after net income such as extraordinary losses and future liabilities are *unique* to each individual company. These items affect earnings so that the earnings number can have more (or less) items or events affecting Company A than those affecting Company B in any one reporting period. Thus, the earnings number does not constitute a good comparison number.

The earnings number is unique to each individual company because the earnings number contains items that *do not lend themselves to the predictability* of future earnings.

Since the earnings number is adjusted differently depending on the individual company choices and individual situations or events, it *cannot* be used as a number for comparison between different companies. Thus, it follows that earnings cannot be used as the return number in the ROE ratio when ROE is used as a comparison ratio.

A truer, more comparable number would be earnings *before* extraordinary write-offs and future liabilities, which is, of course, *net income.*

Clean Surplus literature tells us definitely and positively to use net income rather than earnings for the return number in the ROE ratio. In other words, use net income, which is earnings *before* non-recurring items.

This is exactly what the founding fathers of Clean Surplus told us to do: Use net income and not earnings for the return portion of the ROE ratio. So let's do what we're told.

Please remember that the founding fathers of Clean Surplus were trying to develop a statement that showed predictability of the future, and earnings doesn't show predictability if a company has items (non-recurring) on the income statement that do not lend themselves to predictability.

If you agree with this scenario so far, congratulations, because you are already one giant step ahead of most analysts.

SUMMARY

1. Earnings is the return portion of the traditional accounting ROE. However, the earnings number contains non-recurring items, which do not lend themselves to predictability. Therefore, the earnings number is *not* configured the same for all companies and thus cannot be used as a comparison number. And this is why most money managers cannot outperform the averages. They are simply using the wrong return number in the ROE ratio.

2. Net income is the return portion of the Clean Surplus ROE ratio because net income is configured in the same manner for all companies and is, thus, a truly comparable number.

3. Clean Surplus Accounting develops an ROE ratio that can be used as a comparison among all companies because the return number (net income) is calculated in the same manner for all companies.

4. Clean Surplus ROE is absolutely and positively configured the same way for all companies. This is why the followers of Clean Surplus outperform the averages.

Chapter 8

The Equity Portion of the Return on Equity

*N**ote:* The return numbers (both earnings and net income) we just finished discussing are found on the income statement. The book value or owners' equity is found on the balance sheet. The book value or owners' equity supposedly represents the value of the company.

There are two terms we must understand before we go on. You continually hear the terms "book value" and "owners' equity." Let's discuss the definitions.

Book value is defined as "assets minus liabilities." Think of your house. You bought it for $100,000 with a $20,000 down payment. You owe the bank $80,000. The book value of your asset (the house) is the value of the asset, which is $100,000, minus the liability, which is the $80,000 you owe the bank. Your book value (net worth) is, of course, the $20,000 you put down.

> Book value is assets minus liabilities.

Owners' equity is defined as "the amount of equity (money) investors have put into the company." Owners' equity equates to common stock sold by the company plus all the retained profits (earnings after dividends are paid out), which are put back into the company year after year so the company can grow.

Please notice that using the house example, the owners' equity is also equal to the book value of $20,000. It is the amount of your equity money that you put into the house. The problem with accounting is that our example of the house is where the similarity ends between book value and owners' equity.

> Owners' equity is the amount of common stock sold to investors plus profits (or losses) after dividends are paid out.

The definition for book value is different than the definition for owners' equity, but yet we use both terms synonymously on the balance sheet, and they must be numerically equal to each other on the balance sheet. This is a very serious problem and one that we are about to solve with Clean Surplus Accounting.

Let's go back to the income statement once again because the earnings number on the income statement directly affects the book value on the balance sheet.

Income Statement
Revenues
minus all operating expenses including depreciation, interest, and taxes
= Net Income
minus non-recurring items such as extraordinary losses (or gains)
= Earnings

Earnings

There are two primary actions a company can take with earnings. The company, through its board of directors, can decide to give the earnings to the shareholders in the form of dividends, and/or they can reinvest the earnings back into the company so the company can buy more assets and grow. In the instance of reinvesting all or a portion of the earnings back into the company, the reinvested earnings are then called "retained earnings" because the company is retaining the earnings for company use.

Remember from Chapter 7 that the items that appear *after* net income (non-recurring items) on the income statement have no predictive qualities. If this is true, and it is, we will have little or no predictability of the future value (future growth) of our stocks if we use the earnings number to try and determine predictability.

Let's now go to the balance sheet.

Balance Sheet
Assets
minus **Liabilities**
Book Value *or* **Owners' Equity**

You can see that the assets minus the liabilities equals book value or owners' equity. We also know that owners' equity consists of the money brought in from issuing (selling) common stock *plus* all retained earnings. And retained earnings is all the profit ever made by the company over the years, which, has been reinvested back into the company.

In accounting, the link between the income statement and the balance sheet is this retained earnings number. The profit (or loss) from the income statement is brought over to the balance sheet and added to (or subtracted from) book value (owners' equity) under the subheading of retained earnings.

Accounting Statements and the Link between Them

Figure 8.1 is a simplified accounting income statement and balance sheet that shows the link between the two statements. This link makes sense. If you make a profit and put that money back into the company in the

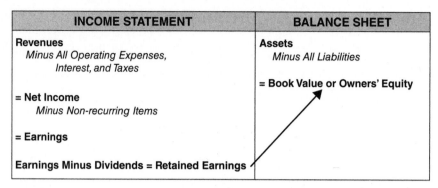

Figure 8.1 Book Value Increased by Addition of New Profits

form of retained earnings, the company now has more value and this increase in value shows up on the balance sheet. The book value (owners' equity) has increased due to the addition of new profit.

> Retained earnings is the link between the income statement and balance sheet.

Ok so far? But we have a really, really *big* problem that has just been carried over from the income statement to the balance sheet.

Remember those non-recurring items unique to the company, which distorted earnings as a comparable number? We said we want to use net income for our return number rather than earnings because net income is figured the same for each company and earnings is not. Net income does *not* include those items that are different for each company. This means that net income is the number that must be used to compare one company to another.

The earnings number, which includes items unique to each individual company, should *not* be used as a comparison number between companies because the earnings number contains items that *are not* part of the normal operations of the company. These non-recurring items *do not* allow for predictability according to Clean Surplus Accounting.

Very important bottom line: If the earnings number is a distorted number for purposes of comparison because of items that are *not* part of ordinary operations, then when the retained earnings number is carried

INCOME STATEMENT	BALANCE SHEET
Revenues *Minus All Operating Expenses,* *Interest, and Taxes* **= Net Income** ———————— *Minus Non-recurring Items* **= Earnings** **Earnings Minus Dividends = Retained Earnings**	**Assets** *Minus All Liabilities* **= Book Value or** ▶ **Owners' Equity**

Figure 8.2   Clean Surplus—The Link Without Distortions

over to the balance sheet, won't book value become distorted and thus not comparable? *Absolutely.*

Yes, I know, pretty heavy stuff. But let's look at an example. Just remember that Clean Surplus uses net income as the return portion of the ROE ratio. And it follows that in order to obtain Clean Surplus retained earnings for the balance sheet, we must subtract dividends only from *net income.* In this way, any distortion in earnings due to non-recurring items *will not* be carried over to owners' equity.

This is Clean Surplus and the link without distortions between the income statement and the balance sheet (Figure 8.2).

This calculation of Clean Surplus retained earnings is one of the two most important segments in the development of predictability as was intended by the accounting profession relative to Clean Surplus.

The General Motors Story

What happened to General Motors? It was a perfect example of the distortion of book value.

Now let's look at an example of how the book value of a company can become extremely distorted when extraordinary events are reflected in its earnings.

At the end of 1991, the stock of General Motors was valued at a book value of $42.89 per share. By the end of 1992, GM's valuation was reduced by a mind-boggling 80 percent to a book value of just $8.47 per share.

General Motors Book Value

1991	1992
$42.89	$8.47

How in the world did GM experience an 80 percent reduction in value in one year? It really didn't, except on paper. GM was forced to account for the *future* medical liabilities of their then present workers upon the workers' retirement. GM was required by FASB (Financial Accounting Standards Board) Statement No.106 to disclose nonpension postretirement benefits, such as health care and life insurance benefits, as future liabilities (see addendum to this chapter). Companies in the same boat as General Motors were required to either take the write-off in equal increments over 20 years or take the total amount of write-off in just one year. GM chose the latter. GM deducted today (1992) only on paper those costs they would incur sometime in the future as their workers retired.

Let's go through the numbers. And of course, I am taking great literary license to simplify the process because GM had negative net income in 1992, which I'm not showing. Since I don't want to cloud the picture, I'm using numbers that are not totally correct, but the theme is the same, and the reduction in value of approximately 80 percent is totally accurate (see Figure 8.3).

Please remember that the future liability was a paper transaction with no cash outflow. The money subtracted from GM's net income actually stayed within the company.

These 1992 negative earnings of −$34.42 must now be carried over to the balance sheet and subtracted from all previous retained earnings,

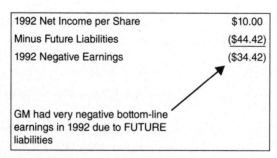

1992 Net Income per Share	$10.00
Minus Future Liabilities	($44.42)
1992 Negative Earnings	($34.42)

GM had very negative bottom-line earnings in 1992 due to FUTURE liabilities

Figure 8.3 Negative Earnings Due to Future Liabilities

which in turn reduced book value (owners' equity) drastically. Let's go there.

1991 Per Share Book Value (Owners' Equity) $42.89
1992 Retained Earnings (this is the big loss)   ($34.42)
1992 New Book Value $ 8.47

Please remember that owners' equity is comprised of the common stock sold by GM and all retained earnings. Since the traditional accounting retained earnings is a negative (−$34.42) in this case, the −$34.42 must be subtracted from the previous total of common stock sold and all previous retained earnings up to this point. In GM's case, book value (owners' equity) was reduced by a whopping 80 percent to just $8.47. Also remember that this situation was not common to all companies.

Clean Surplus *does not allow* this discrepancy to occur. Why? You can see in Figure 8.4 that if the Clean Surplus retained earnings (net income, *top arrow*) was carried over to the balance sheet, then the −$34.42 paper loss *would not have affected* owners' equity. This is because the huge future liability paper loss occurred *after* net income in the income statement.

However, by using traditional accounting earnings or earnings *after* non-recurring items as the tie-in between the income statement and balance sheet (*bottom arrow*), the negative $34.42 must be carried over

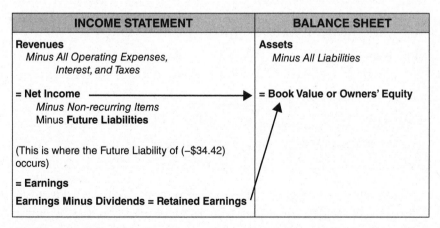

Figure 8.4   Why Clean Surplus Does Not Allow Discrepancies Resulting from Future Liabilities

to the balance sheet, and will in turn absolutely and totally and forever distort book value (owners' equity).

This future liability and the manner in which it was accounted for was unique to GM (and some other companies) at that particular time, and this event will (and did) distort the book value of GM forever into the future right up until its bankruptcy.

The Central Flaw of Traditional Accounting

In traditional accounting, the future liabilities and other non-recurring items *first distort earnings* as a comparison number, and then this distortion, which is included in retained earnings, is carried over to the balance sheet where it then *distorts the owners' equity or book value* as a comparable number. Thus, *both* traditional accounting earnings *and* traditional accounting book value now contain an item that *shows no predictability* because it is a one-time write-off and is unique to a particular company at a particular time in the life of that company.

Let's Not Forget the Main Question

The main question becomes this: Did the assets of GM really decline by 80 percent practically overnight? No, they weren't reduced at all. The money stayed in the company. After all, this was a non-cash event. In the future, it will be a cash event over many years as workers retire, but today, nothing changed. However, the balance sheet showed that the book value or owners' equity was reduced an unimaginable 80 percent to just $8.47 per share with just the stroke of an accountant's pencil.

> Traditional accounting is very complicated. Clean Surplus is as clean and simple and pure as newly fallen snow.

The equity portion of the traditional accounting ROE has been greatly distorted by a unique event that artificially distorted earnings, which in turn greatly distorted (and artificially reduced) book value (owners' equity). This did not happen to most other companies at that particular time.

Bottom line: The distortion caused by non-recurring items in the traditional accounting earnings results in a distorted *retained* earnings number being carried over to book value. Accounting book value (owners' equity) then becomes distorted (not comparable) in each individual company.

If this is true, and it is, then we've lost the second part of the ROE equation in that the book value (owners' equity) from the balance sheet is not configured the same way among all companies because of individual events, which are unique to individual companies.

This leads us to the conclusion that we cannot use either traditional accounting earnings or traditional accounting book value as comparable numbers in our ROE calculation.

Addendum to The General Motors Story

For those of you who are interested in the future liabilities issue of General Motors and other companies, here's something you might be interested in.

Let us visit the actual ruling that caused GM's write-down in accounting book value. The following is quoted from a published dissertation (Belmonte, "Clean Surplus Accounting: Relevance of Earnings and Book Value," Nova Southeastern University, 2002):

> An example of a drastic change in book value from one year to another resulted in a change in the balance sheet book value of General Motors from $42.89 in 1991 to $8.47 in 1992 as reported by Value Line. Value Line's footnote attributed the drop in book value to a nonrecurring loss.

A page from *Accounting: Text and Cases,* Ninth Edition by Robert Anthony explains the drop in book value for General Motors to an accounting concept.

> Beginning no later than 1993, companies are also required by FASB Statement No. 106 to make disclosures of **nonpension postretirement benefits**, such as health care and life insurance benefits. Formerly, such expenses were recognized on a pay-as-you-go basis. Now, the substance of accounting for

these benefits is similar to that for pensions: The total costs that will be incurred by retirees is estimated and a portion of the present value of these costs is charged as an expense in each year that an employee works. For health care costs, this requires estimating employees' needs for postretirement health care services as well as the future cost of such services. These are even more difficult and uncertain estimates than those required for pensions.

For many companies this requirement resulted in identification of a huge obligation for previously unfunded and unrecognized future nonpension postretirement benefits that employees already had earned.

Companies were given the choice of treating this obligation either as (1) a change in accounting principle (described later in this chapter), with the entire obligation treated as an expense of the period in which the change was made; or (2) on a delayed basis, amortizing the obligation on a straight-line basis over the average remaining service period of active plan participants or 20 years, whichever is longer. Many companies elected the first, "one-big-hit" approach; as an extreme case, for General Motors this approach reduced 1992 net earnings by $20.8 billion ($33.38 per share).

Until they were required to do so by FASB 106, many companies had not estimated the overhanging burden of future health care benefits. This led some companies to reduce such benefits, which in some cases led to labor disputes.

The two sources quoted here do not agree on the book value of GM. Value Line shows the decrease in book value to be $34.42, while *Accounting: Text and Cases* shows the write-down to be $33.38. However, a basic question arises. Did a drop of approximately $34 (almost 80 percent) per share in accounting balance sheet book value actually change the asset base upon which GM manufactures cars?

SUMMARY

Traditional accounting book value (owners' equity) includes in its calculations all the items (from traditional accounting retained earnings) that are unique to that individual company. Thus, traditional accounting book value (owners' equity) is not configured the same for each company. Since book value (owners' equity) is not configured the same for each company, it *cannot* be used as a comparable statistic.

This leads us to the conclusion that we cannot use either traditional accounting earnings or traditional accounting book value as comparable numbers in our ROE calculation.

Chapter 9

How to Determine an Equitable Equity Number

The last several pages were pretty heavy in one way, but on the other hand, the concept is very much just plain common sense. Look at it this way: You are just one step away from being able to develop a portfolio that will outperform most of those professional money managers out there in Investment Land: *just one step away.* Once you are finished with this book, the adoption of Clean Surplus into your stock portfolio will indeed seem second nature. And as I said to myself when I first learned the system, "This is so easy, why didn't I think of this method myself?"

Let's Review Just a Bit

Previously we learned that we could not use earnings as a comparable number between different companies. This was because the earnings number becomes distorted as a comparable number due to unique, non-recurring

INCOME STATEMENT	BALANCE SHEET

Revenues
  Minus Expenses
	Assets
	  Minus Liabilities

= Net Income Minus Non-recurring Items (Such as Extraordinary Losses and Future Liabilities)	**= Book Value (Owners' Equity)** (Common Stock + All Retained Earnings)
= Earnings	
Earnings – Dividends = Retained Earnings	

Figure 9.1 Earnings and Book Value Distorted by Non-Recurring Items on Income Statement

items on the income statement (Figure 9.1). These non-recurring items certainly must be accounted for, but in no way do they allow for the predictability that the investment community so dearly seeks.

We also learned that if the earnings number is distorted as a comparable number due to the non-recurring items, then book value (owners' equity) also becomes distorted as a comparable number between companies. The earnings number from the income statement directly affects book value on the balance sheet because retained earnings (earnings minus dividends) is the tie-in between the two statements. Thus, one distortion keeps on distorting. Or, one bad apple spoils all the others.

Bottom line: Neither traditional accounting earnings nor traditional accounting book value (owners' equity) can be used as comparable numbers. Thus, the traditional return on equity (ROE) ratio, which consists of both traditional accounting earnings and traditional accounting book value, cannot be used as a comparison ratio. Eat your heart out, Wall Street.

We've already solved the problem of the return portion of the ROE ratio. Rather than using earnings, we use net income as our return number (Figure 9.2). Net income is configured the same among all companies and is thus a comparable number.

However, we still have a problem with book value (owners' equity), which we are about to solve right now. Just remember that net income does not equal earnings when there are non-recurring items in the equation. Somehow we must standardize the book value (owners'

INCOME STATEMENT	BALANCE SHEET

Revenues
  Minus Expenses
	Assets
	  Minus Liabilities

= Net Income Minus Non-recurring Items (Such as Extraordinary Losses and Future Liabilities) **= Earnings**	**= Book Value (Owners' Equity)** (Common Stock + All Retained Earnings)

Figure 9.2   Net Income Used as Return Number

equity) number, so we can develop a Clean Surplus ROE that allows us to compare one company to another.

Our New Return on Equity Equation

In order to find a comparable book value or owners' equity, we must develop a book value (owners' equity) in the same manner as we did with our bank accounts. In other words, we must develop a Clean Surplus book value (owners' equity).

The return (earnings) on equity (book value) from the accounting statements cannot be used as a good comparison ratio.

Between 1895 and 1937, there was concern in accounting circles of the inability of accounting statements to predict the operating efficiency and thus the future value of a company.

The discussion centered on how the accounting numbers should show what investors needed to know about a company and at the same time allow for some sort of *predictive capability*.

The result was a surplus accounting statement showing earnings before abnormal charges or non-recurring items (extraordinary write-offs and future liabilities), which is, of course, net income. Thus, in Clean Surplus Accounting, net income becomes the "return" number for the ROE calculation.

Book value or owners' equity is not as easy. Surplus accounting, which was later called Clean Surplus Accounting, calculates its own

Table 9.1 Bank A and Bank B—Beginning with $100

	Bank A			Bank B		
Year	Equity	Interest	ROE	Equity	Interest	ROE
5	$146.00	$14.60	10.00%	$142.45	$11.40	8.00%
4	$133.00	$13.30	10.00%	$131.29	$11.00	8.50%
3	$121.00	$12.10	10.00%	$120.45	$10.85	9.00%
2	**$110.00**	**$11.00**	10.00%	$110.00	$10.45	9.50%
1	**$100.00**	**$10.00**	10.00%	$100.00	$10.00	10.00%

owners' equity true to the definition of owners' equity. Remember, owners' equity is the common stock issuance plus all retained earnings.

But Clean Surplus distinctly says that the only addition to the retained earnings account on the balance sheet should be net income (minus dividends) from the income statement.

We can now begin to understand and use the true definition of owners' equity: the common stock issuance plus all retained earnings. According to Clean Surplus, these retained earnings can only come from net income (minus dividends).

Let's examine two separate bank accounts (oh no, not again!), each beginning with $100 (Table 9.1). Let's also assume all interest (net income) is reinvested back into both accounts.

Owners' equity is defined as the amount of money the owners put into the bank account plus all the retained interest. Don't forget, the interest (net income) belongs to the owners. Since the interest is retained in the bank account, it is called "retained" interest (retained earnings).

This bank example shows how simply Clean Surplus works. Owners' equity of today equals owners' equity of last period plus the retained profits at the end of the last period.

In Clean Surplus Accounting, retained profits is net income (minus dividends). Or, how much money with which we began the year plus how much we earned (and retained) gives us next year's beginning balance.

Yes, Clean Surplus Accounting is this simple because it is *clean*. It is clean because we *do not* include in our calculations any future liabilities or extraordinary write-offs or any non-recurring items, which *do not* lend themselves to predictability.

We actually use Clean Surplus to figure the yearly returns on our bank account and our stock accounts. It's a wonder analysts don't use it to figure the return on a company's assets. Of course, those who read this book will use it. And after you finish this book, you will use it forever.

Looking to the bank account examples in Table 9.1, we can see that the ROE for Bank A is a constant 10 percent. However, Bank B, because of some unknown reason, shows an ever-decreasing ROE.

Note: We don't care what the reason is that the ROE of Bank B is decreasing. All we want to know as investors is which bank is the better bank relative to operating efficiency? Clean Surplus ROE is a bottom-line number that tells us which company is being more efficient about its operations. The Clean Surplus ROE tells us which companies should be in our portfolio and which companies should be in somebody else's portfolio.

The question for us to answer is very simple: All else being equal, which bank would you rather put your money in?

And the second question is equally simple: Why can't we use the bank account method in the same manner with individual companies as well as our bank accounts?

We can use the bank account example and we will because Clean Surplus Accounting allows us to do so. And you will see that Clean Surplus Accounting is the concept that makes us different from the rest of the investment world.

What Does Warren Buffett Say about All This?

What does Warren Buffett say about the shortcomings of accounting book value? He simply says that accounting book value is meaningless as an indicator of a firm's intrinsic value.

I don't know about you, but Buffett pretty much says in just one sentence what I've been trying to get across to you for the past nine chapters. And I'll spend several more chapters showing you how Clean Surplus works in the real world.

SUMMARY

1. Clean Surplus distinctly tells us that the only addition to the retained earnings account comes from net income (minus dividends) and not the traditional earnings (minus dividends).

2. Clean Surplus uses the true definition of owners' equity as the book value (owners' equity). How much money did the company begin with through common stock sales and how much was added through retained profits? Thus, not only is net income configured the same among all companies, but because Clean Surplus uses net income (minus dividends) to add to book value (owners' equity), then book value (owners' equity) is also configured the exact same way among all companies *and is thus comparable among all companies.*

3. However, the entire world uses the traditional accounting book value in their ROE calculation as a comparison model. This is why most of the entire world cannot outperform the market averages. They don't know an efficient method of comparing the operating efficiency of one company relative to another company. But we do!

Chapter 10

The Predictability of Finance Valuation Models

L et's leave the numbers and ratios once again and give our minds a much-needed rest. So on the lighter side, I think it would be a good time to discuss the differences between the fields of accounting, finance, and investments.

The intention of this book is to negotiate the complicated worlds of accounting and finance using a bit of common sense. Common sense is especially useful when it comes to superior stock selection for our own personal portfolios. Accounting has its ratios, and finance has its valuation models. Neither discipline works nearly as well as Clean Surplus when it comes to analyzing and comparing the operating efficiency of one company relative to the operating efficiency of another company. The word "compare" is the Holy Grail of the investment world and is only able to be calculated through the implementation of Clean Surplus.

You see, accounting is just as the word implies. It is a system that accounts for almost everything that happens to and/or within a company. And we need accounting. I am not saying that accounting should be changed, nor am I criticizing accounting. I need it and you need it. It's just that we need something a bit more understandable and easier to work with when trying to determine the operating efficiency of a company. And the accounting profession understands that. After all, it was the accounting profession that developed Clean Surplus in order to solve this problem. So yes, accountants, thank you very much.

Finance is different from accounting. The world of finance uses the numbers from accounting to make future financial decisions for the company. Finance attempts to answer questions related to capital structure such as the optimal debt to equity ratio that should be maintained in a company. Capital structure is the amount of money borrowed through issuing bonds (and other types of debt) relative to the amount of money raised through the issuance of common stock.

Finance also determines which of the many projects a company should invest in for maximum return to the company and its shareholders. This process is part of the capital budgeting process. Capital budgeting also must consider the proper amount of money invested into each project, the cost of capital, and how to raise that capital. So yes, there is a lot to the world of finance.

Then there is the world of investing. Many people think finance is investing. Let's trash this common belief before you become affected (infected) by it. Investing is forgoing gratification today for the potential of even greater gratification in the future. Thus, investing is the discipline that must be able to determine which companies are capable of giving us the greatest and most consistent gratification over the long term.

Accounting is different from finance, which is different from investing. Accounting and finance were developed to work *within* the company, while investing must be able to rise above a particular company and compare an overall operating efficiency measure *between* many companies.

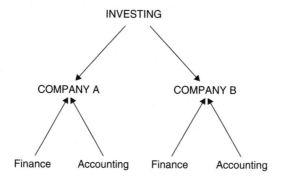

Figure 10.1 The Worlds of Investing, Finance, and Accounting

The accounting and finance disciplines were developed and continue to be developed to work *within* the company. Investing, on the other hand, deals with the comparison of one company to another (Figure 10.1). Since each company is unique, it is very difficult to accomplish this comparison using systems that weren't designed for comparison.

This inability of effectively comparing the operating efficiency of one company to another shows itself in the very few number of investment managers who are able to outperform the averages on a fairly consistent basis. Remember, only about 4 percent of money managers can consistently outperform the market averages over a 10-year period on a risk-adjusted basis.

Efficiency Is the Key

In order to invest in the stock market, you must master the science of selecting a portfolio of companies that are more efficient in their operations than the other companies out there in investing land.

There are three things you need to know about a company:

1. How efficient that company is in generating profits.
2. How consistent that company is relative to the generation of profits over many time periods.
3. How efficient other companies are in both areas so that you are able to compare them in order to select the most efficient and the most consistent companies for your portfolio.

The ratio most widely used to determine operating efficiency is the traditional accounting ROE ratio. But we know the traditional accounting ratio doesn't work very well for comparison of different companies. In order to get on with your investing life you want to be able to tell the difference between the traditional accounting ROE and the Clean Surplus ROE. As we go on to the next several chapters, you will see Clean Surplus in action, and you will understand even more why you *want to use clean surplus return on equity only,* just as we did with our bank accounts.

There is a huge disparity between the traditional accounting ROE and the Clean Surplus Accounting ROE, and mastering that disparity becomes the difference between outperforming the market and not outperforming the market. Trust me on this one.

College and Finance Valuation Models— They Just Don't Work Very Well

As we learned earlier, there is a big difference between accounting, finance, and investing. The problem is that the academic world doesn't understand there is a difference between investing and the disciplines of accounting and finance. In fact, most of the investing world is not aware of the difference between investing and finance. How do I know this? The investment world continues to hire portfolio managers with finance backgrounds and guess what? They cannot outperform the market averages on a continual basis. So folks, something is wrong with this picture.

The various finance valuation models, which we will take approximately one or two seconds of our lives to discuss, were all developed with finance and not investing in mind. And guess what? They don't work very well as investment tools. Let's go on and see if what I say is true.

In business schools across the country, we teach our students various stock valuation models, which were developed in order to determine the present and supposedly true value of a company. After all, if we were able to determine the true present value of a company through the models, we could simply compare the model value of the company to the price the stock is presently selling for in the open market.

If a stock is selling for $50 a share and we determine, through one of the multitude of models, that it is presently worth $100 a share, we should immediately run out and buy as much of that stock as we possibly can. We can then go to the beach and wait until the market participants realize the stock is so greatly undervalued. Once this discrepancy in calculated value relative to the present price is discovered, everyone will then buy the stock until it reaches its full valuation of $100 a share. By that time, we'd be very rich because we originally purchased it for $50 a share. See how this works so well in the world of fantasy?

What are these valuation models? Well, you asked, so I shall tell you. We have several versions of the dividend discount model: no growth, steady growth, and variable growth. Please let us not forget the capital asset pricing model (CAPM), which calculates expected returns based on a measure of risk known as beta. What? Then there are the discounted cash flow models, such as the sum of the discounted cash flows and the sum of the discounted "free" cash flows. Of course, for any of these models, there may be several definitions for each variable within the model.

"Whoa, stop, HOLD IT!!! What do you mean by several definitions of each variable within the various models? I don't even know what a variable is. What's going on here?"

I once attended a financial conference in Orlando, Florida. An academic gave an excellent lecture on Economic Value Added (EVA). For his research article, he polled executives from the Fortune 500 company list to ask their perception of the meaning of EVA. He received 168 different definitions. The same is true of some of the academic models.

Different meanings within the same model? Here's a quick example. I mentioned "beta." Beta is a measure of risk. Roughly it is how a stock moves relative to the market.

For example, let's say the market moves up 10 percent and your stock moves up 5 percent or 15 percent or down 10 percent at the same time the market moves up 10 percent. Beta tells us this relationship of movement relative to the market. The beta of the market is one. If a stock has a beta greater than one, it supposedly has a higher risk (higher volatility) than the market. In turn, we expect the stock to return more than the return of the S&P 500 or Dow. If we take more risk, we expect a greater return.

Value Line calculates beta by using weekly data over a period of five years. One of the large brokerage companies calculates beta using monthly data over a five-year period. And I have no idea over what time frame one of the on-line services calculates beta.

All I know is that at any one time, the beta for a single company is different, depending on the time frame used for the calculation of that company's beta. If this is so, and it is, how in the world can one use beta in a calculation and come up with a reasonable answer? The answer is *you can't*. Everyone involved in the calculation process will use different betas, depending on their source of beta, and of course, will come up with different answers.

Hey, my students continually give me different answers on tests, and they are all using the *same* beta. And don't forget, my students are the future money managers of the world.

I can give you a very simple reason why I know these financial models don't work. If any of them did work, wouldn't all the academic professors of the world be as rich as Buffett?

How does Buffett view the academic models? Buffett pretty much feels that his position as the greatest investor ever is secure as long as our business schools continue teaching the models they now teach along with something called the "efficient market hypothesis." So what does Buffett do? Read on.

You see, the models don't work very well for stock selection, and as a result, most of the money managers out there cannot outperform the averages. So we must determine for ourselves a nice simple method that we can use to select good companies for our portfolios. And this book gives us that method.

You see, not all analysts spend their lives futilely trying to determine the true value of a company. Some of them try to determine which companies earn a comparably high return on their asset (equity) base. If we can determine a proper model for return on equity, we should be able to compare the operating efficiency of one company to that of another. *The market will eventually reward the more efficient companies.* And we want to own these companies. Period.

> The market will eventually reward the more efficient companies.

Bottom line: Let's not try and fool ourselves into believing that we should spend a lot of time trying to find a good valuation model, since none has yet been found since the beginning of time. Rather, let's try to find a very simple method of determining which companies are consistently more efficient in their operations than other companies. The more efficient a company is, and the more consistent that company is in generating profits, the greater will be our reward if we own stock in that company.

You are off to a good start in formulating a stock selection process, but there is more to the story. After all, if this were all you had to learn, this chapter would be the last chapter. We must now learn *how* the comparison process works. We must also learn how Buffett uses the process to determine a proper purchase price. And finally, we must learn about the predictability of the ROE as calculated by Clean Surplus Accounting. Yes folks, your financial future is contained in the next several chapters.

SUMMARY

1. Accounting is different than finance, which is different than investing.
2. The valuation models just don't work very well. If they did, all the professors who teach finance would be as rich as Buffett.
3. The key to investing is to find the companies that are consistently more efficient in their operations than other companies.
4. The market will eventually reward the more efficient companies, and these efficient companies are the companies we want to have in our portfolios.

Chapter 11

Clean Surplus ROE—
the Only Comparable
Efficiency Ratio

Developing the Tools to Determine the
Probability of Predictability

Y ou are now aware of a very straightforward method for calculating a return on equity that is truly common to all stocks. We
are calculating both the return (net income) and the owners'
equity the same way for each individual stock. We are comparing apples
to apples and peaches to peaches.

Let's review by thinking once again of the bank account examples
shown in Table 11.1. The account of Bank A is earning more money in
year five ($14.60) because it has a higher equity (asset) base ($146). How

Table 11.1 Bank A and Bank B—Beginning with $100

	Bank A			Bank B		
Year	Equity	Interest	ROE	Equity	Interest	ROE
5	$146.00	$14.60	10.00%	$142.45	$11.40	8.00%
4	$133.00	$13.30	10.00%	$131.29	$11.00	8.50%
3	$121.00	$12.10	10.00%	$120.45	$10.85	9.00%
2	$110.00	$11.00	10.00%	$110.00	$10.45	9.50%
1	$100.00	$10.00	10.00%	$100.00	$10.00	10.00%

did Bank A accumulate a higher equity (asset base) than Bank B when both began year one with the same amount of equity? Because Bank A earned a greater return on its asset base. Since it earned a higher return *and* reinvested all the interest back into the account, Bank A was thus able to retain more dollars than Bank B.

Now here's the ultimate, most important, mind-shattering, earth-shaking saber-rattling question in the entire world of investing. If you had the opportunity to buy the assets of the account in Bank A or the assets of the account in Bank B, which account would you be required to pay more for?

Now you are beginning to understand why some stocks sell for more than other stocks. They are earning more. Why are they earning more? Because they are generating a higher return on a larger and faster increasing asset base through the reinvestment of their earnings. And if they have done this consistently in the past over a long period of time, we might logically expect them to continue to do so in the future.

My stocks are worth more than your stocks because I pick stocks with a high and very consistent ROE (Clean Surplus Accounting), and my stocks retain more profits and thus build the asset base faster than your stocks. The larger the asset base, the more products it can produce. The more products, the more sales. The more the sales, the more profits. The greater the profits, the higher the value of the company. Period!

If I must compare one company with another as to greater operating efficiency, I have a very simple and practical method to do so. And now, so do you.

Clean Surplus

We are about to embark on real-life examples with both General Electric and General Motors. Since the time I gave these examples in the first edition of this book, General Electric went through a very tough period, and General Motors went bankrupt. We will revisit both these companies in Chapters 13 and 14 where we will bring these companies up to date. We will show you when and why we sold General Electric, and we will tell you why we never would think of buying General Motors. Please notice the dates on these stocks as they *are not* up to date in this chapter. They will be brought up to date later.

OK everybody, ready to analyze real stocks? Let's begin with General Electric shown in Table 11.2. We begin our analysis with book value from January of 1986. Why 1986? 1986 just happened to be the first year for which I had data, and we would like to have at least 10 years of data so we can see if the stock exhibits a pattern of consistency.

Table 11.2   General Electric (GE)

Year	Owners' Equity	Net Income	Dividends Paid	Retained Earnings	Return on Equity
2002	$7.16	$1.65	$0.72	$0.93	23.05%
2001	$6.39	$1.41	$0.64	$0.77	22.08%
2000	$5.67	$1.29	$0.57	$0.72	22.76%
1999	$5.09	$1.07	$0.49	$0.58	21.03%
1998	$4.58	$0.93	$0.42	$0.51	20.32%
1997	$4.11	$0.83	$0.36	$0.47	20.21%
1996	$3.70	$0.73	$0.32	$0.41	19.75%
1995	$3.33	$0.65	$0.28	$0.37	19.54%
1994	$3.00	$0.58	$0.25	$0.33	19.35%
1993	$2.71	$0.51	$0.22	$0.29	18.84%
1992	$2.48	$0.42	$0.19	$0.23	16.96%
1991	$2.22	$0.43	$0.17	$0.26	19.39%
1990	$1.97	$0.40	$0.16	$0.24	20.43%
1989	$1.75	$0.36	$0.14	$0.22	20.72%
1988	$1.56	$0.31	$0.12	$0.19	20.04%
1987	$1.41	$0.27	$0.11	$0.16	18.95%
1986	$1.28	$0.23	$0.10	$0.13	17.70%

We begin with book value (owners' equity) from the balance sheet, which is the traditional accounting book value we are all familiar with. The academic research terms this "dirty" book value. Why do we begin with dirty balance sheet book value? It's easier than going back to 1888 or so (yes, GE is a very old company) and trying to find beginning book value (owners' equity). So we begin with dirty book value (owners' equity) and clean it up.

Looking at the very bottom line, we begin by taking 1986 net income (not earnings) of $0.23 and then subtract $0.10 of dividends. This leaves us with $0.13 of retained earnings. We then add the retained earnings ending 1986 ($0.13) to the beginning 1986 book value ($1.28), which gives us beginning book value for 1987 of $1.41 (Table 11.3).

In order to calculate the ROE for 1986, we use the net income of $0.23 (return) and divide it by the book value (owners' equity) of 1986 ($1.28) to obtain return on equity for 1986 of 17.70 percent.

> In Clean Surplus Accounting, net income minus dividends equals Clean Surplus retained earnings.

And to find book value (owners' equity) for the present year, we must add last period's retained earnings (net income − dividends) to last period's book value (owners' equity). Just think of the bank account examples. It's the exact same method. In this case, 1987 book value (BV) ($1.41) = 1986 BV ($1.28) + 1986 Retained Earnings (RE) ($0.13).

$$BV_{1987} = BV_{1986} + (\text{Net Income - Dividends or RE})_{1986}$$

or

$$BV_{1987} = BV_{1986} + (\text{Clean Surplus RE})_{1986}$$

Table 11.3 General Electric (GE)

Year	Owners' Equity	Net Income	Dividends Paid	Retained Earnings	Return On Equity
1987	$1.41	$0.27	$0.11	$0.16	18.95%
1986	$1.28	$0.23	$0.10	$0.13	17.70%

Now you understand why I had you look at the bank account examples so many times. You calculate the book value (owners' equity) and ROE with stocks the exact same way you did with the bank accounts. Yes, it's clean and simple.

Remember, we are going through these calculations so we can calculate the return on equity (ROE). A high and consistent ROE tells us most of what we need to know about a stock.

We are looking to see if the ROE developed from Clean Surplus Accounting lends itself to predictability. Rather than wait, I'll tell you right now. The ROE certainly does indeed lend itself to predictability.

I Forget, What Are We Looking For? Let's Review!

We are trying to find a *comparable* return on equity ROE ratio so that we may compare the operating efficiency of one company to the operating efficiency of any other company. In order to find a comparable ROE for all companies, we must configure both the return (net income) and the equity in the same manner for each and every company. Traditional accounting *does not* allow us to do this. Clean Surplus Accounting absolutely *does* allow us to do this.

The Clean Surplus asset base (owners' equity or book value) is comprised of common stock sold to investors plus all Clean Surplus retained earnings (retained profits). Please remember that the Clean Surplus earnings number is actually net income: or, as they said in 1895, earnings before abnormal charges.

> Please remember that the Clean Surplus earnings number is actually net income or, as they said in 1895, earnings before abnormal charges.

What have we accomplished here? Net income is configured *before* we adjust for *individual, non-recurring* company charges. Thus, net income is calculated the same among all companies up to the point of the non-recurring individual company charges.

Always remember that book value (owners' equity) under Clean Surplus is comprised of the money the company raised through common stock sold to investors plus all Clean Surplus retained earnings. Clean Surplus retained earnings is net income minus dividends.

If owners' equity is calculated in the same manner for all companies, then both the owners' equity and net income (from which owners' equity is derived) are common among all companies. If this is true, and it is, then the ROE ratio as configured by Clean Surplus Accounting is truly a comparable method of determining operating efficiency. And most importantly, this method is common to all companies.

I'm sorry if I sound like I'm repeating myself, but I'm trying to make sure you understand the basic premise of investing, which is evidently lost on most professional money managers. Ok, here we go.

Let's now look at just the ROE of both General Electric and General Motors (GM), with the ROE configured using Clean Surplus Accounting shown in Table 11.4. We are looking only at the Clean Surplus ROEs for our comparison. Please note these ROEs stop at 2002 for this example.

Table 11.4   GE and GM ROE

	GM ROE	GE ROE
Average	**7.4%**	**20.6%**
2002	3.4%	22.4%
2001	4.7%	22.1%
2000	13.5%	22.4%
1999	15.2%	21.0%
1998	9.9%	20.3%
1997	16.8%	20.2%
1996	13.4%	19.7%
1995	19.9%	19.5%
1994	19.9%	19.3%
1993	7.1%	18.8%
1992	−13.4%	17.0%
1991	−19.0%	19.4%
1990	−7.6%	20.4%
1989	12.6%	20.7%
1988	14.8%	20.1%

> Return on equity as configured by Clean Surplus Accounting is truly a comparable method of determining operating efficiency.

When using Clean Surplus Accounting, we see that GE has a high average ROE (20.6 percent) and a relatively consistent ROE, while GM has a low average ROE (7.4 percent) and a very *inconsistent* ROE. Again, please be aware that both ROEs were configured using Clean Surplus Accounting (bank account example), and not the traditional accounting ROE that we are so familiar with.

When you consider that the ROE is a measure of operating efficiency, we come to an age old question: If this were 2001 and you were looking at these numbers, would you rather invest in a very efficient company such as GE, or would you rather invest in a very inefficient company such as GM?

Remember that the market hates inconsistency. We see that General Motors has a negative ROE of 19 percent in 1991 and a positive 19.9 percent in 1994. In some years it is making a lot of money and in some years it is losing a lot of money.

Now look at General Electric. The ROE is high and very consistent, with a bias toward an increasing ROE. The market *loves* consistency, and the market rewards those companies that have a high and consistent ROE.

In the 10 years prior to 2002, GE stock increased from a split adjusted $6 per share to $24 per share for a 300 percent increase, not including dividends. During the same time period GM's stock went from $35 to $33 for a loss except for dividends. Well, I guess what I said is true about the market rewarding a high and consistent ROE.

> The market loves consistency, and the market rewards those companies with a high and consistent ROE.

What you have discovered is a truly comparable method of determining operating efficiency. And this method is common to all companies.

The question we will answer a bit later in this book is whether the ROE is an indication of the future return of a portfolio. It certainly looks to be the case with GE and GM up to 2002.

Bottom line is if the ROE is an indication of the future returns, we can then fill our portfolios with stocks that have high and consistent ROEs and the rest will take care of itself. The answer to the question of ROE being an indicator of future returns will make you smile.

When we bring these two companies up to date in Chapter 14, you will see there was a time when GE just had to be sold.

SUMMARY

1. In Clean Surplus Accounting, net income minus dividends equals retained earnings:

$$BV_{1987} = BV_{1986} + (\text{net income} - \text{dividends})_{1986}$$

or

$$BV_{1987} = BV_{1986} + (\text{Clean Surplus retained earnings})_{1986}$$

2. Return on equity, as configured by Clean Surplus Accounting, is truly a comparable method of determining operating efficiency.
3. The market loves consistency, and the market rewards those companies with a high and consistent ROE.

Chapter 12

What Buffett Looks for in a Company, or How Clean Surplus Accounting Recognizes the Quality of a Company

I personally believe the numbers eventually tell us almost all we need to know about a company. My research work and my continual model portfolio results demonstrate the usage of numbers in valuation. It is my belief that most money managers think too much. They feel they must know everything there is to know about a company.

I, on the other hand, believe you don't have to know whom the CEO plays golf with. I don't believe you must know if the company has a day care center for the workers, or if they have special parking spaces, or if the company has a politically correct working atmosphere.

The reason I don't worry about all of this is because if a company is doing everything right, then it will eventually show itself in the bottom-line numbers. It will show up in the return on equity (ROE) as configured by Clean Surplus Accounting.

However, for now, let's leave the numbers behind while we delve into the *qualitative* aspects of a company that Warren Buffett looks for in a "good" company.

Qualitative simply translates into those aspects (qualities) of a company that in many instances cannot be measured with specific numbers on the income statement or balance sheet. I just want you to remember as we go over this area that the ROE as configured by Clean Surplus Accounting "accounts" for almost everything we are about to discuss. In other words, I believe that all the good (or bad) "stuff" that the analysts normally look for in a company eventually flows down to the bottom line and shows itself sooner or later in the operating efficiency (ROE) as configured by Clean Surplus.

So remember as we go through this chapter that it is my belief that all the subjective and qualitative aspects of a company eventually expose themselves in the bottom-line numbers such as the Clean Surplus ROE. However, let's look at these qualitative aspects of a company, so we can begin to understand the common sense reasoning behind why some companies have a high and consistent ROE and other companies fail to achieve that high and consistent ROE.

Buffett

Buffett is known as a value investor. It is difficult to understand why Buffett has been termed a value investor and not a growth investor. Once you begin to understand Buffett, you will soon determine he is actually a growth investor buying growth stocks at a very good value. This point is well proven through the use of Clean Surplus ROE. Let's discuss the types of businesses Buffett might consider for his portfolio. And it is these specific types of businesses that have the ability (with good and honest management) to possibly exhibit a high and consistent Clean Surplus ROE.

The Consumer Monopoly versus the Commodity Type of Business

Buffett divides the investment world into two main categories. He classifies these categories as the good and profitable consumer monopoly types of businesses and the not-so-profitable commodity types of businesses. Once Buffett identifies a consumer monopoly company, he begins his financial calculations. If he decides to add a particular security to his portfolio, he will wait for an adverse market, industry, or individual company condition to misprice that security and give him his predetermined purchase price.

Buffett is well known for his extraordinary patience. It is this patience that has rewarded him so very well over the years because he knows all too well that sooner or later he will be able to buy the stock of his choice at his predetermined price. Think of his involvement in Heinz in 2013. I read an article that said Buffett had been looking at Heinz for over 20 years.

The Commodity Type of Business: Companies Buffett Avoids

A commodity type of business is a business that manufactures and/or sells a non-differentiated product that is also manufactured and sold by one or several other companies. The airlines, car manufacturers, and producers of cyclical products such as steel, oil, gas, and lumber are considered commodity companies by Buffett. In other words, a commodity type of business has considerable competition in the marketplace. For the most part, a commodity type business has very little or possibly no product differentiation except price. Please be aware not to confuse product differentiation with effective marketing or advertising.

Because there is little or no product differentiation and because of immense competition, the main weapon employed by a commodity type of business is price reduction. As competition enters the market, prices must be lowered. As prices are lowered, profit margins may become almost nonexistent.

> Little product differentiation and intense competition lead to low profit margins.

However, commodity businesses do well when the economy is doing well. During an economic expansion, the demand outpaces supply, and companies such as the auto manufacturers can make a lot of money. However, when the economy is not doing so well, these companies will fall from grace in a very short period of time.

Let's look at Table 12.1 that shows the ROE of General Motors once again up to 2001. You can see that the ROE is very inconsistent. Some years, such as 1990 through 1992, GM had a negative ROE, which means the company was losing money. As you are all aware, the market hates when a company loses money three years in a row or even in just one year. When you see this type of inconsistency, you are usually looking at a cyclical and/or commodity type of company.

Another shortfall of the commodity type of business is that it must use most of its profits to upgrade its manufacturing equipment in order to stay competitive. Thus, a company of this type cannot use the

Table 12.1   General Motors: A Cyclical Company

	ROE
2001	2.6%
2000	10.7%
1999	15.2%
1998	9.9%
1997	16.8%
1996	13.4%
1995	19.9%
1994	19.9%
1993	7.1%
1992	−13.4%
1991	−19.0%
1990	−7.6%
1989	12.6%
1988	14.8%

majority of its profits to increase the size of its manufacturing asset base. It must use profits just to remain competitive and upgrade the present asset base. If a company cannot *add* to its asset base, it cannot increase sales. If it cannot increase sales, it cannot increase earnings per share. If it cannot increase earnings per share, the price of the stock will not increase.

General Motors was actually losing market share during the period shown here. (Of course, we now know it continued to lose market share right up to its bankruptcy in 2009.) Because GM was losing market share, we know GM's retained earnings were *not* being used to increase the size of the asset base. The question, of course, is why would anyone invest in a company that was losing market share and was *not* increasing the size of its asset base?

If retained earnings are not being used to increase the asset base, how can we expect earnings to increase? We can't!

Still yet another shortfall is the heavy debt load of many of the commodity type of companies. Think again of General Motors. General Motors had approximately 77 percent long-term debt relative to total capitalization in 2003. GM could take all its profits for the following 10 years and still not pay off its debt. Of course, we now know GM did not last another 10 years. When it declared bankruptcy in 2009, all of the common stock became worthless and new stock had to be issued.

These are the types of companies Buffett avoids. They are not consistent in their earnings and, for the most part, they cannot use retained earnings to grow the company, but instead must use their retained earnings just to stay competitive.

> The main weapon a commodity type of company can use is price reduction.

How else can we identify these types of companies? They are identified by intense competition due to multiple companies producing the same product with very little brand loyalty toward that product. When demand slacks off, the only weapon these companies have against one another is price reduction.

> Price reductions lead to lower profits. Lower profits lead to lower
> share prices.

Price reduction, in turn, leads to lower profit margins, lower return
on shareholders' equity, and very inconsistent earnings.

The Consumer Monopoly: The Type of Business Buffett Loves

A consumer monopoly is a business that is entirely opposite of the commodity type of business. We can think of many companies that have
brand loyalty or have had brand loyalty in the past.

When you were younger and were thirsty, you had a Coke. When
you thought about chocolate, you asked for a Hershey bar. When you
thought of a record player (yes, I remember record players), you thought
of RCA. As you grew older and began to shave, you thought of Gillette.

Has competition come into the market for some of these products? Certainly. Has the market changed the need for certain products?
Certainly. Does anyone have a record player any longer? We have an entire generation who at this moment has no knowledge of vinyl records.
But did RCA make several generations happy and did several generations
of investors obtain great wealth by investing in RCA? I certainly know
this to be true. Yes, consumer monopolies can last many, many years.

When a company develops brand loyalty for their particular product, they are building the goodwill of their company. Goodwill can add
a great deal of value to a company and, as a stockholder, you certainly
know this to be a good thing. If you think back to the commodity type
of businesses, you will be hard-pressed to find a steel company (commodity type of company) with as much goodwill built into its stock
price as Coca-Cola or Heinz or Colgate.

> A consumer monopoly has brand loyalty.

Sometimes it is difficult to determine a consumer monopoly from a product alone. However, once we look into the financials of a company, we will be able to determine who is building a consumer monopoly and which consumer monopoly is losing its luster. We delve into the financials in other chapters, but for now, let's look at the attributes that identify the consumer monopoly.

> Brand loyalty adds goodwill to a company.

A consumer monopoly will have an identifiable product or service. The company will probably maintain a low debt margin. Low debt is particularly important because if a company is generating a good profit, it is able to reinvest that money in order to build its investment (asset) base, upon which it can earn still more profits which means its stock price will eventually increase. It is better to use profits to increase a company's asset base rather than using profits to pay interest on debt.

> Goodwill adds to the value of the company.

If a company must enter into the debt markets, it very probably means it is not generating enough profits to grow the company sufficiently to warrant it a long-term investment. Buffett would much rather own a company with a little debt than a lot of debt.

> Low debt is a good thing.

Here are four important questions to ask:

1. Does the company earn a high return on shareholders' equity? In other words, is the company efficiently using the equity investors have invested in the company? Would you rather put your money in a bank paying interest of 10 percent or a bank paying interest of 5 percent?
2. Does the company then use its retained earnings (profits reinvested back into the company) to grow its asset base and thus grow the company?

3. Is the company earning the same high ROE on the newly invested equity (retained earnings) as it did on its previously invested equity?

4. If the company is not adding to the asset base with retained earnings, is the company using that money to add value to shareholders by repurchasing some of its own outstanding shares?

Buying back shares allows profits to be distributed among fewer outstanding shares, which means more profits per outstanding share. This, of course, increases the value of the remaining outstanding shares, which is a good thing for the remaining shareholders.

In conclusion, the Clean Surplus ROE alone will tell us almost everything we just discussed in this chapter. Yes, the Clean Surplus ROE is that good.

> Bottom line: A high ROE tells us the company is using its retained earnings in an efficient manner.

SUMMARY

A well-run growth company will use its retained earnings to grow its asset base. The more the asset base grows, the more products the company is able to produce. The more products produced, the more sales are able to increase. The more sales, the more profit. The more profit, the higher the ROE. The higher the ROE, the higher the value of the stock. And folks, that's what this is all about.

1. A commodity type of business has lots of competition and very little product differentiation.

2. Little product differentiation and intense competition lead to low profit margins.

3. If retained earnings are not being used to increase the asset base, how can we expect the earnings to increase in the future? We can't.

4. The only weapon a commodity type of company can use is price reduction. Price reductions lead to lower profits. Lower profits lead to lower share prices.
5. A consumer monopoly has brand loyalty.
6. Brand loyalty adds goodwill to a company.
7. Goodwill adds to the value of the company.
8. Low debt is a good thing.
9. A high ROE tells us that the company is making efficient use of its asset base.
10. The Clean Surplus ROE tells us most of what we need to know about a company.

Chapter 13

General Electric Then and Now

How Buffett Uses Clean Surplus Accounting to Determine the Future Target Price and the All-Important Purchase Price, or Buy Low and Sell High

The Purchase Price

Everyone knows the key to making money in the stock market is to buy low and sell high. In the past, we didn't have a clue as to what was high and what was low. In this chapter, you will learn how to calculate both a purchase price and a sell price in order to obtain your long-term required return. After all, this is how Warren Buffett became one of the richest individuals in the world.

In this chapter, I will show you how, according to Mary Buffett and David Clark in their book *Buffettology*, Warren Buffett determines a "target" price and a "purchase" price. A slight problem is even Mary and David don't know that Warren Buffett uses Clean Surplus Accounting. But thank you, Mary and David, for showing the world the target price and purchase price calculations.

Warren Buffett uses Clean Surplus Accounting to determine the level of operating efficiency (return on equity, or ROE) and the consistency of that operating efficiency. The more consistent a company is in its operating efficiency, the better he (or anyone) is able to predict a future price. If he can effectively predict a future price, he can then determine when the value (market price) of the company gets to a low enough level (purchase price) that will generate *his* required return over the next decade. The difference between his purchase price and his target price is his profit.

Possibly the most unique aspect of Warren Buffett is that he is extremely patient. He selects his security purchase price very, very carefully. Then he waits and waits until an opportunity arises that presents him with this previously calculated purchase price.

Patience

I don't think there is another person in the world who is as patient as Buffett. How can he be so patient? He has other uses for his cash while he is waiting for the "right" price. For one thing, he engages in arbitrage. And he is not opposed to buying preferred stock, which will pay him a very nice return for the use of his cash. In other words, he knows what to do with his "idle" time and money.

Most of us do not have the time (nor the cash) to learn and then put into action what Warren does so successfully with his short-term cash. All we can do for the moment is determine what he does with his long-term cash, which is invest in good growth stocks at a good value (price). Or we can just determine what the best stocks are, buy them, and let the very good company managers continue their good work. The market eventually recognizes good work, and our good stocks will give us a very nice profit.

What is meant by management performing "good work" in a growth company? First of all, we want management to earn a very good return on shareholders' equity. Second of all we want to see most or all of that profit being reinvested back into the company and then generating an equally good return on that reinvested capital. Just think of a bank account that is paying 10 percent per year consistently year after year. All we have to do as investors is search out these stocks.

We will construct a superior performing portfolio with those stocks that will allow us a greater predictive ability in a later chapter. For now, let's look at examples and practice using those examples. Let's see how Warren Buffett uses Clean Surplus Accounting to determine when a company represents a good value (Table 13.1).

Back to Basics

Bank Account A is acting very much like a bond. It is returning 10 percent per year on our money. If we owned a bond paying 10 percent and were able to reinvest our interest payments also at a rate of 10 percent, we would have Bank Account A.

If the bond paid 10 percent per year for the past 10 or 15 years, we could make a pretty good assumption that the bond may very well return 10 percent to us over the next 10 years.

Table 13.1   Bank A and Bank B

	Bank A			Bank B		
Year	Equity	Interest	ROE	Equity	Interest	ROE
Year 15	$378.00	$37.80	10.00%	????	???	???
5—the present	$146.00	$14.60	10.00%	$142.45	$11.40	8.00%
4	$133.00	$13.30	10.00%	$131.29	$11.00	8.50%
3	$121.00	$12.10	10.00%	$120.45	$10.85	9.00%
2	$110.00	$11.00	10.00%	$110.00	$10.45	9.50%
1	$110.00	$10.00	10.00%	$100.00	$10.00	10.00%

The problem with the stock market is common stocks are just not as consistent as bonds. However, it is our job (not that difficult) to find the companies that do indeed earn a fairly consistent return on the invested equity capital.

A Very Important Point

Notice the amount of money in the account of Bank A in year five. It is $146. We began year one (five years previously) with just $100. Therefore, $46 of the $146 is retained interest (retained earnings).

What is so important is that in year five, Bank A is returning 10 percent on the entire $146. This means that Bank A is earning 10 percent on the original $100 and also earning 10 percent on the reinvested capital of $46.

In other words, Bank A is earning a high return on the *reinvested* capital as well as the original capital.

Look at Bank B. It is earning an ever-lower rate of return on the money in the account. This is not a good sign. It means that Bank B is not deploying its new (reinvested) capital as efficiently as Bank A nor is it earning the same rate of return on its reinvested capital as it did in previous years.

Back to the Good Bank

If we assume that the bank (or bond, or stock) will pay us 10 percent per year for the next 10 years, and we are reinvesting all of that money back into the account (retaining 100 percent of earnings), then we can, with some degree of accuracy, project out and estimate how much money we will have in Bank A 10 years from now (Table 13.1, repeated here).

Table 13.1   Bank A and Bank B

	Bank A			Bank B		
Year	**Equity**	**Interest**	**ROE**	**Equity**	**Interest**	**ROE**
Year 15	**$378.00**	**$37.80**	**10.00%**	**????**	**???**	**???**
5—the present	$146.00	$14.60	10.00%	$142.45	$11.40	8.00%
4	$133.00	$13.30	10.00%	$131.29	$11.00	8.50%
3	$121.00	$12.10	10.00%	$120.45	$10.85	9.00%
2	**$110.00**	**$11.00**	10.00%	$110.00	$10.45	9.50%
1	**$110.00**	**$10.00**	10.00%	$100.00	$10.00	10.00%

How do we do this? We begin with the amount (equity) we have in Bank A in year five (the present time), which is $146. We know, or are assuming with a certain degree of confidence, that the future rate of return on our capital will continue to be 10 percent. We know we are retaining all that we earn. Thus, we project this $146 out for 10 years at the growth rate of 10 percent.

Only if you're really interested, the actual calculation is: $146 × (1 + (0.10 × 1.0) ^ 10). It is the amount of $146 which we multiply by 1 plus the interest rate (10 percent or 0.10) times the retention rate (reinvested rate) of 100 percent (or 1.0) all raised to the 10th power. The 10th power represents compounding over the time period of 10 years.

Of course, we use a computer spreadsheet, put the formula in once, and save the formula to all the stocks in my program database. Got to love computers.

This calculation gives us the amount of money (equity) we will have in Bank A 10 years from now. If we know with some certainty the amount (asset base) we will have in the bank in year 15 ($378), and we assume our rate of return is still going to be 10 percent, we can then calculate our interest (net income) in year 15 which is 10 years from now.

The earnings or interest we will earn in year 15 will be the amount we have in the bank in year 15 ($378) times the 10 percent which we feel Bank A will still be earning for us at that time. Ten percent times $378 gives us interest (net income) of $37.80, which is the amount we estimate we will earn in year 15 in Bank A.

The Account of Bank B

Let's look at the account of Bank B. It has a decreasing rate of return. The big question is how in the world will we be able to figure out what we will have in the bank in year 15 (10 years from now) if we don't know what the rate of return on our invested money will be over the next 10 years? The answer is we don't know. We don't have a good consistent rate of return upon which we are able to base our projections. If we can't make a good assumption because of inconsistency, then why even think of investing in Bank B when Bank A is just around the corner? And yet some people will invest in Bank

B because they feel somehow, by some grace of Lady Luck, it will turn around and earn much more than Bank A or because they like the name of the company or they heard something positive from a friend or . . . .

Watch that word "turnaround." Buffett has been heard to say that turnarounds seldom turn. Why even take the chance? Especially when you have no clue as to the probability of a turnaround. Buffett loves probabilities, and yet he won't take many chances like that, so why should we?

Beware, Beware, Beware

I want to use two stocks I used in several of my university classes many years ago. They are General Electric (GE) and General Motors (GM). These are both great examples because General Electric eventually fell from grace, and General Motors eventually went bankrupt.

We will use the original numbers and dates here, and we will bring these two companies up to date later. Do not use the following data as a guide as whether or not to invest in these companies. However, GE and GM were such good examples back in the day (one good and the other bad) that I want to use them here so you will be aware that long-term holding does not mean forever. Long-term holding means that you buy a good stock and hold it until it is not a good stock any longer. This was indeed the case for General Electric. The case for General Motors is you never should have bought this stock in the first place. Even the blind kid (in Chapter 14) knew not to buy this stock way back in 1999.

Just to let you know, we sold GE at the very beginning of 2004, and we will show you why as we go along.

A Real Stock

Let's look at a real stock (Table 13.2).

Table 13.2   General Electric—NYSE GE

Year	Projected OE	Net Income	10-Yr. Avg. P/E Ratio	10-Yr. Target Price	Required Return	Buy Price
2012	$21.15	$4.35	23	$100	12.6%	$31

Year	Owners' Equity	Net Income	Dividends Paid	Retained Earnings	Return on Equity	10-Year Average ROE	Retention Rate	10-Year Average Retention
2002	$7.14	$1.60	$0.72	$0.88	22.4%		55.0%	
2001	$6.37	$1.41	$0.64	$0.77	22.1%		54.6%	
2000	$5.67	$1.27	$0.57	$0.70	22.4%		55.1%	
1999	$5.09	$1.07	$0.49	$0.58	21.0%		54.2%	
1998	$4.58	$0.93	$0.42	$0.51	20.3%		54.8%	
1997	$4.11	$0.83	$0.36	$0.47	20.2%		56.6%	
1996	$3.70	$0.73	$0.32	$0.41	19.7%		56.2%	
1995	$3.33	$0.65	$0.28	$0.37	19.5%		56.9%	
1994	$3.00	$0.58	$0.25	$0.33	19.3%		56.9%	
1993	$2.71	$0.51	$0.22	$0.29	18.8%	20.6%	56.9%	55.7%

We see that GE had a pretty consistent ROE right up until 2002. In fact, the ROE was steadily increasing, which is a very good thing. The most important aspect of these calculations is that the more consistent a stock's ROE, the more accurate our projections will be.

> The most important part of all these calculations is the more consistent a stock's ROE, then the more accurate our projections will be.

Buffett likes to take averages over periods of 10 years. He will take the past 10-year average of the ROE, which in the case of GE is 20.6 percent.

The next question: Is GE putting all of its earnings back into the company? The answer is no. It is paying some of the earnings out in the form of dividends. Net income minus the dividends gives us the Clean

Surplus retained earnings or the amount of the net income GE is putting *back* into the company.

Net income – dividends = Clean Surplus retained earnings.

The retained earnings is the amount of money from earnings put back into the company each year. However, in order to compare one company to another company when it comes to the amount of money put back into the company each year, we use a ratio called the "retention rate."

In order to calculate the retention rate, we simply divide the retained earnings by the total net income.

Retention rate = retained earnings / net income.

For 2002 (see Table 13.3), retained earnings of $0.88 divided by net income of $1.60 ($0.88/$1.60) gives us a retention rate of 55.0 percent. The retention rate is the *percentage* of the earnings (net income) retained or put back into the company. You can see this in the retention rate column.

Table 13.3 General Electric (GE)—Retention Rate

Year	Owners' Equity	Net Income	Dividends Paid	Retained Earnings	Return on Equity	10-Year Average ROE	Retention Rate	10-Year Average Retention
2002	$7.14	$1.60	$0.72	$0.88	22.4%	20.6%	55.0%	55.7%

Buffett then takes the average retention rate of, you guessed it, the past 10 years, which is 55.7 percent (Table 13.4).

Table 13.4   General Electric (GE)—Retention Rate—10 Yr. Avg. ROE

Year	Owners' Equity	Net Income	Dividends Paid	Retained Earnings	Return on Equity	10-Year Average ROE	Retention Rate	10-Year Average Retention
2002	$7.14	$1.60	$0.72	$0.88	22.4%	20.6%	55.0%	55.7%

Let's catch up here for a moment. GE has an average 10-year ROE of 20.6 percent. Of that amount, GE has averaged, over the past 10 years, a retention rate of 55.7 percent. So we know GE's 10-year ROE on invested equity (20.6 percent) and how much of those earnings that GE is retaining (55.7 percent) or putting back into the company. Remember, these are all 10-year averages.

Why does Buffett use 10-year averages? I don't know, but it could be that over any 10-year period, the economy goes through recessions and also economic expansions. As the economy goes through these cycles, expectations about a company's future will rise and fall with the mood of all of us. Thus, he probably feels that over a 10-year period, we see the average of at least one complete economic cycle, and of course, the ensuing mood swings that accompany both the good and bad times. Hey, makes sense to me.

The P/E Ratio

Speaking about mood swings, the price-to-earnings (P/E) ratio reflects these mood swings. The price-to-earnings ratio reflects investor expectations about the future earnings of the company, and these expectations rise and fall with the performance of the economy, both actual and perceived.

Back in the late 1990s during the dot.com-era, everyone was happy and investors expected earnings to go to the sky. The growth of some stocks was expected to rise exponentially (like, way above the sky). These fantastic expectations were reflected in the very high P/E ratios at that time.

Then around 2002 as well as 2008, the mood shift had taken a 180-degree turn. Everyone was focused on all the negatives in the world, and that mental depression was being reflected in the stock market. The news seemingly could not get any worse, and people were selling into each

> The price-to-earnings ratio reflects investor expectations about the future earnings of the company, and these expectations rise and fall with the performance of the economy, both actual and perceived.

and every rally. As stock prices declined, the P/E ratio declined because of very low expectations.

The bottom line on the P/E ratio is that it represents a certain multiple of earnings for which the stock is selling. This multiple is different for each company and each industry and each cycle in the economy (whew!). The P/E ratio is based on the price of a stock that reflects the *perceived* growth of earnings, either up or down for whatever reason or reasons.

Please be aware that the P/E ratio is configured differently by the different reporting sources. One source uses present price relative to the trailing 12 months of earnings, while another source will use the past six months of actual earnings and the next six months of its own projected earnings. Many other sources use future earnings based upon present price. Again, beware of which P/E people are referring to.

> Different sources calculate the P/E ratio in different ways. Value Line uses recent price divided by the latest six months' earnings per share plus estimated earnings for the next six months. Other sources use the trailing 12 months' earnings while other sources use future earnings.

Back to the Future

Please remember to look at the spreadsheet of GE as I go on with the numbers. We discussed how to obtain a future earnings projection. Just reviewing a bit, we take the owners' equity of 2002 ($7.14) and project that out 10 years by using the return on that equity (past 10-year average of 20.6 percent) times the retention rate (past 10-year average of 55.7 percent). This calculation gives us 2012 owners' equity of $21.15 (Table 13.5).

In order to obtain 2012 net income, we multiply 2012 owners' equity ($21.15) by the past 10-year average of ROE (20.60 percent), which gives us 2012 net income of $4.35.

Once we calculate 2012 net income, we then multiply the net income ($4.35) by the past average 10-year P/E ratio (23) to give us our *expected* price in 10 years of $100. ($4.35 × 23 = $100). This $100 becomes our approximate 10-year projected target price.

But now we must discount the future price of $100 back to the present (2002) in order to determine a proper purchase price. Let's see how we do this.

Table 13.5 General Electric GE

	Projected OE	Net Income	10-Yr. Avg. P/E Ratio	10-Yr Target Price	Required Return	Buy Price
2012	$21.15	$4.35	23	$100	12.6%	$31

Year	Owners' Equity	Net Income	Dividends Paid	Retained Earnings	Return on Equity	10-Year Average ROE	10-Year Retention Rate	10-Year Average Retention
2002	$7.14	$1.60	$0.72	$0.88	22.4%		55.0%	
2001	$6.37	$1.41	$0.64	$0.77	22.1%		54.6%	
2000	$5.67	$1.27	$0.57	$0.70	22.4%		55.1%	
1999	$5.09	$1.07	$0.49	$0.58	21.0%		54.2%	
1998	$4.58	$0.93	$0.42	$0.51	20.3%		54.8%	
1997	$4.11	$0.83	$0.36	$0.47	20.2%		56.6%	
1996	$3.70	$0.73	$0.32	$0.41	19.7%		56.2%	
1995	$3.33	$0.65	$0.28	$0.37	19.5%		56.9%	
1994	$3.00	$0.58	$0.25	$0.33	19.3%		56.9%	
1993	$2.71	$0.51	$0.22	$0.29	18.8%	20.6%	56.9%	55.7%

Let's Discount Back—the All Important Purchase Price

Once we obtain the 10-year future target price, we can then discount that future price back to the present.

What? We just forecasted a price 10 years out; why do we want to get back to the present?

We've got to figure out the purchase price or value at which we want to purchase the stock today. You see, if we can assume with a fair degree of certainty what the future price will be in 10 years, we still must calculate the price to purchase today, which will generate for us our required return. And that purchase price is based on the *return we require* per year over the next 10 years.

This is such an important concept and represents the pure genius of Warren Buffett. Everyone in the entire world is trying to put a value on a stock, and of course as I've mentioned several times before, the academic pricing models do not work very well, if at all. If they did work, all the professors in all the universities who teach these models would be as rich as Buffett, and they're not.

You see, by using Buffett's method, we are not putting a value on the company relative to its worth (we can't); we are putting a value on a stock relative to what it is worth *to us*. We should purchase GE at a price of $31 per share today *if we want a total return of 15 percent per year,* which would include 2.4 percent in dividends and 12.6 percent in stock appreciation.

> The more consistent the stock in the past, the more comfortable we are with our projections for the future.

Remember that old saying, buy low and sell high? Well, we just figured out the high price, which is the 2012 target price. Now, we've got to figure out the purchase price, which is the "low" part of that very famous saying.

Let's say we desire a 15 percent rate of return. Why did I say 15 percent? Well, in a case study of Warren E. Buffett found in Robert Bruner's *Case Studies in Finance*, he (Bruner) suggests that Buffett's required rate of return is 15 percent. So let's use 15 percent.

Let's use General Electric once again. Back in 2002, GE was trading at approximately $29. It was paying a dividend of $0.72 a share, which represented a 2.4 percent dividend return. Thus, if we want a 15 percent per year return, we are already receiving 2.4 percent in dividends. Therefore, the stock must appreciate (price increase only) just 12.6 percent per year (15% − 2.4%). Please remember that a stock's total return is price appreciation *plus* dividends.

In order to calculate our purchase price, we must put the required return of 12.6 percent in the required return box of our spreadsheet or the computer program that accompanies this book. The computer will automatically discount back the future price 10 years at the rate of 12.6 percent, and give us a buy price of $31 (see Table 13.6).

If you really need to know the formula, it is the future price ($100) divided by 1.126^{10}. Or the future price divided by 1 plus our required return of 12.6 percent (0.126) raised to the 10th power. The 10th power represents the number of years we are discounting back. Yep, 10 years.

As you can now see, the purchase price of GE should be approximately $31 per share. This means that if GE continues to generate a return on equity of approximately 20 percent and continues to reinvest approximately

Table 13.6   General Electric (GE)—Buy Price

	Projected OE	Net Income	10-Yr. Avg. P/E Ratio	10-Yr Target Price	Required Return	Buy Price
2012	$21.15	$4.35	23	$100	12.6%	$31

Year	Owners' Equity	Net Income	Dividends Paid	Retained Earnings	Return on Equity	10-Year Average ROE	10-Year Retention Rate	10-Year Average Retention
2002	$7.14	$1.60	$0.72	$0.88	22.4%		55.0%	
2001	$6.37	$1.41	$0.64	$0.77	22.1%		54.6%	
2000	$5.67	$1.27	$0.57	$0.70	22.4%		55.1%	

56 percent of those earnings back into the company for growth, the 10-year future price (target price) should be approximately $100 per share. Discount the future price of $100 per share back by 12.6 percent (required appreciation), and we obtain a purchase price of $31 per share.

Bottom line here is if the assumptions are correct, and in the past they had been up to 2002, and we could purchase GE at $31 a share, we should see GE at approximately $100 a share 10 years from 2002. This price appreciation plus the dividends will generate a total of 15 percent yearly rate of return for us.

Now you understand the importance of the purchase price. The purchase price is the basis for the return that a stock will generate for us over the next 10 years.

> The all-important purchase price determines what our total future return will be, which equates to price appreciation plus dividends.

Important Note: Approximately

As you can see, I use numbers like 12.6 percent and $100 target price and retention rate of 55.7 percent. Please don't get hung up on the decimal places or exact numbers. Buffett says that it is better to be approximately correct than precisely wrong. The future of the economics of the world, country, and individual company can only be approximated. If the past has been consistent, then we are assuming the future will be consistent. So "approximately" is the word of the day.

The other side of the market (other than economics) is the human emotion. I can tell you this with exactness. Human emotion can take those precise numbers and make them all look rather silly.

Put both economics and human emotion together and think about this for a moment. Think about how much you were worth in 1999 and how much you were worth at the end of 2002. I would say your worth was not *exactly* the same.

So maybe you might think about how I handle the situation and do what Warren Buffett suggests. It's better to be approximately correct than precisely wrong. And I leave it at that.

Very Important Addendum

The last three short paragraphs have proven to be extremely important since I last wrote them. The financial crisis of 2008 has proven to be very long lasting to say the least.

General Electric changed part of its business model in that it became very involved with financing and, as with most companies, GE was susceptible to swings in the worldwide economy. Over the years, the economies of the world have become more and more correlated. What this means is what happens in the United States also happens around the world.

Let's bring the GE numbers up to the present time (Table 13.7) and see where we would have sold it using the Buffett and Beyond rules of investing.

Table 13.7   GE ROE
to Present Date

	ROE
2015	10.8%
2014	10.4%
2013	10.6%
2012	10.4%
2011	9.4%
2010	8.7%
2009	8.0%
2008	14.4%
2007	19.5%
2006	19.3%
2005	18.1%
2004	**18.5%**
2003	**19.5%**
2002	22.4%
2001	22.1%
2000	22.4%

1. We want stocks in our portfolio that have Clean Surplus ROEs of 20 percent or greater.
2. We will sell a stock when the ROE falls below 20 percent.

Pretty simple, isn't it? There are a few more basic rules which we'll cover later, but just these two rules will help you structure a portfolio which will in all probability outperform 96 percent of professional money managers of the world. Again, pretty simple.

Up to this point, we've been showing GE up to 2002. However, in 2003, the ROE dropped below our threshold of 20 percent. The difficult question becomes this: Is half percent below 20 percent worth selling a stock that had been so very consistent in the past? The same thing happened to AutoZone in that the ROE dropped slightly below 20 percent, and AZO came back and continued to be a stellar stock.

However, 2004 saw GE's ROE continue to drop, and if you didn't sell in 2003, you surely had to sell in 2004 according to our guidelines.

GE continued to be pretty good for the next three years from 2005 to 2007, but then the ROE began to decline drastically until it began to recover slightly into 2011. The company is beginning to come back, but it seems as though this company will never be the generator of earnings that it once was. As things look at the present time, GE will probably never again grace our growth portfolio. However, it may be a candidate for our income portfolio, which we will discuss in the Chapters 21, 22, and 23.

The lesson here for a growth stock? When a company changes for the worst, it will show up in the Clean Surplus ROE sooner or later, and then it is time to replace the company with the declining ROE for a company with a nice, high ROE.

SUMMARY

1. The key to purchasing a stock at your required rate of return is patience. A lot of *patience.*

2. The two most important elements of all our calculations are the level and consistency of a stock's ROE. The higher the level of ROE, the greater the expected return on that stock. The more consistent a stock's ROE, then the more accurate will be our overall projections.

3. The price to earnings ratio (P/E) reflects investor expectations about the future earnings of the company, and these expectations rise and fall with the performance of the economy, both actual and perceived.

4. The more consistent the stock's ROE in the past, the more comfortable we are with our projections for the future.

5. If we cannot accurately project the future price due to past inconsistency of their growth in earnings, we cannot discount back to the present in order to determine a proper purchase price. And in Buffett's world, the purchase price is all-important.

6. The all-important purchase price determines what our total future return will be. Total return equates to price appreciation plus dividends.

7. The modern-day followers of Clean Surplus ROE do not try to determine a value for a company. But they do value the company relative to the total return they themselves require from that company over the next 10 years.

Chapter 14

General Motors
Then and Now

The Blind Kid Gives His Opinion

We are not able to determine the future price and present purchase price with companies that have very erratic Clean Surplus returns on equity (ROEs). General Motors (GM) is a prime example of a cyclical company with a very inconsistent ROE. This means the market does not know how to calculate a value for this company. It also means we cannot predict a future price. If we cannot predict a future price, then we cannot determine a good purchase price.

Let's Look at General Motors

General Motors was once part of the Dow Jones 30 Industrials. However, the story on GM is different from that of General Electric (GE). General Motors is a cyclical stock. How do we know this even if we didn't know anything at all about GM? Let's take a look (Table 14.1).

These numbers go up to 2009 (2009 was an estimation for the entire year), which is the year GM went bankrupt. We can see that GM had six years from 1990 to 2009 when it lost money. The negative ROE tells us the company had negative earnings. When you look at GM this way and knowing what you know now, is there any reason you would have bought this stock? After you read Chapter 16, you will see there were (and still are) hundreds of stocks in the S&P 500 index that had high ROEs. Many of those stocks had both high and consistent ROEs, which means there are always plenty of stocks from which you are able to structure a winning portfolio.

And please remember what Warren Buffett says. Look at the ROE. The ROE will tell you all you need to know about earnings.

High ROE

We are looking for a high and consistent ROE. First let's discuss the high ROE. Just what is a high ROE? The ROE of the two most widely used market averages, the Dow 30 industrials and the S&P 500, is

Table 14.1   General Motors (GM)

Year	ROE	Year	ROE
2009	1.51%	1999	15.23%
2008	−3.03%	1998	9.93%
2007	−0.47%	1997	16.83%
2006	5.75%	1996	13.38%
2005	−7.99%	1995	19.91%
2004	8.97%	1994	19.89%
2003	7.36%	1993	7.14%
2002	5.00%	1992	−13.44%
2001	2.63%	1991	−19.02%
2000	10.68%	1990	−7.63%

approximately 14.5 percent. We want to fill our portfolio with stocks that have a higher ROE than the average of 14.5 percent. If we can achieve this (easy), we should be able to structure a portfolio that out-performs the market averages over any four-year period. In Chapter 16, based on my dissertation research, the results covering the S&P 500 show that, over the time period of the study, all the portfolios structured with ROEs higher than the average ROE of all the stocks in the S&P 500 outperformed the market averages over the following four-year time periods. *I said ALL the portfolios.*

By the way, one of the differences between investing and gambling is investing means putting the odds on your side. In order to outperform the averages, we want to put the odds on our side. Thus, we must begin with a superior performing portfolio (above average ROE) as config-ured by Clean Surplus Accounting.

The average 10-year ROE of General Electric was a bit over 20 percent up to 2002. The ROE of General Electric is certainly above the market average of 14.5 percent for the years up to 2002. General Motors, on the other hand, had an average ROE of 4.6 percent for the years 1990 through 2009. This ROE is much, much lower than the market averages. Out of the two stocks, General Electric had been the more efficiently operated company as measured by Clean Surplus ROE up to 2002.

Consistency Up to 2002

The next aspect of ROE we want to consider is consistency. We can look at the ROE of General Electric over time and see that it looked relatively consistent up to 2002 with a bias toward an increasing ROE. However, we really don't know what consistent is. And consistent could really fall in the eye of the beholder. But one thing we can do is compare.

Look at the ROE of General Motors. I'm not sure what the defini-tion of inconsistent is, but I see GM in 1994 with an ROE of over 19 percent, which is good; but then in 1998 the ROE was 9.9 percent, in 2001 down to 4.7 percent, and 2002 even lower. As I said, I'm not sure what inconsistent is, but I'm pretty sure the ROE of GM would fit the bill.

What does "inconsistent" mean relative to the accuracy of our projections? For one, we have a very poor chance of accurately projecting the owners' equity 10 years into the future. We really have no idea what the ROE will be over the next 10 years. In the past, the ROE has been all over the place, and "all over the place" seems very inconsistent to me. If the ROE has been very inconsistent in the past, we can assume it will be very inconsistent in the future. General Motors eventually went bankrupt. How's that for inconsistent?

If we cannot project the equity into the future with any degree of accuracy because of great inconsistency, we certainly cannot project the future earnings. If we cannot project the future earnings, then we cannot project the future price.

Here comes the important part. If we cannot project the future target price with any degree of certainty, we cannot discount back to the present to determine a proper purchase price. And in Buffett's world, the purchase price is all-important.

Yes, our computer program does give us a purchase price for GM (not shown), but the question becomes one of probabilities. What is the probability that the future numbers are anywhere near accurate when GM has exhibited very inconsistent numbers in the past? Inconsistency does not breed accuracy.

> If we cannot accurately project the future price due to past inconsistency, we cannot discount back to the present to determine a proper purchase price. And in Buffett's world, the purchase price is all-important.

Compare

Let's review our findings (Table 14.2).

General Electric had a high and relatively consistent ROE up to 2002, and the ROE had been increasing up to that point. General Motors had a low and very inconsistent ROE. The really big question becomes which stock would you rather have in your portfolio? Let's ask the blind kid.

Table 14.2   GM versus GE

	GM	GE
Avg. ROE	7.4%	20.6%
Year	**ROE**	**ROE**
2002	3.4%	22.4%
2001	4.7%	22.1%
2000	13.5%	22.4%
1999	15.2%	21.0%
1998	9.9%	20.3%
1997	16.8%	20.2%
1996	13.4%	19.7%
1995	19.9%	19.5%
1994	19.9%	19.3%
1993	7.1%	18.8%
1992	-13.4%	17.0%
1991	-19.0%	19.4%
1990	-7.6%	20.4%
1989	12.6%	20.7%
1988	14.8%	20.1%

The Blind Kid—A Sea Story

I want to share with you a little sea story. This story will help you think about avoiding stocks with an inconsistent ROE.

Whenever I want my students to remember an important point, I tell them a sea story to help them along. It falls in the category of learning by association. What is a sea story? A sea story is one that may not be totally correct. Sort of like the "fish that got away" story.

I was the first director of the Student Managed Investment program at a university on the water in Palm Beach, Florida, in 1999 and 2000. Hey, I agree. Lucky me. But just remember the definition of luck. When opportunity meets preparation.

One of the students in my class was blind. Actually, he could see if he put something directly against his face, but he was declared legally blind. You know, I really respected that kid, but that's yet another sea story.

When I showed overhead projections on a screen, I would give him a copy of the projection sheet, which I had enlarged (a lot) prior to class so he knew what was going on during our classroom sessions. I must say, he had better listening skills than most.

We continually had guests coming to our class, as it was a pilot program and several businesses from the community donated money in order to sponsor the project. Several of the "important" people visiting our class from time to time were involved with trust departments run by the area banks. I don't have to tell you that most of them had General Motors in their portfolios. How do I know? Many of them showed me the stocks on their master lists from which they used to select stocks for their clients' portfolios.

I would give my best presentation when guests came to visit. I would perform a complete analysis and comparison on both GE and GM upon which we had numbers projected into 2001. Finally, just to be a little critical and a little antagonistic, I would ask the blind kid about GE and GM.

I would call out in my most sincere and authoritative teaching voice, "Hey Billy, tell me about General Electric and General Motors."

My visually impaired student would always sit in the seat directly in front of me. When I asked this question, he would smile from one ear to the other. You see, no one paid much attention to the blind kid, so here was his chance to shine. He would smile, shake his head from side to side, and say, "General Electric should be in our portfolio, and General Motors should be in somebody else's portfolio."

A Lesson to Be Learned

Of course, you know what I'm going to ask you. If a blind kid could see the difference, then what's your problem?

I mentioned previously that over one of my test periods prior to the year 2000, GE appreciated 300 percent while GM actually depreciated slightly except for dividends over that same time period. Looking at the differing ROEs of both stocks, we are beginning to see that the level and consistency of the ROE seems to have a direct relation to the future total returns. The ROE of General Electric was much higher than the ROE of General Motors and, in turn, General Electric returned a much higher total return over the years relative to General Motors.

Why had General Electric been such a good performer? I don't know. Why had General Motors been a serious underperformer? I don't know, and I really don't care. General Electric had been in my portfolio up to 2004, and General Motors was in someone else's portfolio.

Always remember the good, the bad, and the ugly: The good stocks should be in our portfolios; the bad stocks should be in someone else's portfolio; and the ugly stocks should be in nobody's portfolio.

If you remember the good, the bad, and the ugly, you will forever have a darn good portfolio that should be outperforming 96 percent of those professional money managers out there in Investment Land.

So You See, Folks

You see, folks, the ROE tells us so very much about a stock. In a previous chapter, we discussed many of the qualities Buffett looks for in a stock. Well, I can tell you one thing right now. If the ROE is not high and consistent, then you shouldn't even think about going any further in your analysis on that stock. A high and consistent ROE should be your very first filter in analyzing a stock. End of story!

OK, I will tell you why certain analysts recommended General Motors from time to time prior to bankruptcy in June of 2009. General Motors was and still is (the new GM) a cyclical stock. It doesn't make much money in bad times, but in good times, it can make a lot of money. So if you can time the cycles, then you can do well with a stock like GM.

But always remember this. Most of the money managers cannot outperform the averages on a yearly basis. Out of those who do outperform in one year, there is a 67 percent chance they will NOT outperform the following year. So you tell me. Who out there is in cycle with the cycles?

Addendum to the General Motors Saga

Let's look once again at the ROE of GM right up to bankruptcy (see Table 14.3).

When a company goes bankrupt, all of the common stock becomes worthless. The creditors (mostly bondholders) fight over the remaining assets of the company. If the company filed for reorganization bankruptcy,

Table 14.3   ROE for GM

Year	ROE	Year	ROE
2009	1.51%	1999	15.23%
2008	−3.03%	1998	9.93%
2007	−0.47%	1997	16.83%
2006	5.75%	1996	13.38%
2005	−7.99%	1995	19.91%
2004	8.97%	1994	19.89%
2003	7.36%	1993	7.14%
2002	5.00%	1992	−13.44%
2001	2.63%	1991	−19.02%
2000	10.68%	1990	−7.63%

the common stock becomes worthless, and the company will then issue new stock.

Now let's look at GM after reorganization in Table 14.4.

We can see there is a big difference in the efficiency of the operation of the company. GM has shed a lot of the expenses it had relative to salaries and retirement benefits. At one point just prior to bankruptcy, it was reported that GM had expenses of $1,600 more per car due to medical, retirement, and salary expenses than did Honda and Toyota cars manufactured here in the United States. Whatever the causes for expenses, it is fair to say that GM is doing much better than it did in the past. We can see that the ROE is still not consistent, and the ROE calculations in our table do not include a recession. Only time will tell if GM is able to eventually become a viable company.

Table 14.4   GM after Reorganization

Year	ROE
2015	16.5%
2014	11.9%
2013	13.5%
2012	14.3%
2011	23.5%
2010	21.2%

SUMMARY

1. The key to purchasing a stock at your required rate of return is patience. A lot of *patience*.
2. The two most important elements of all our calculations are the level *and* consistency of a stock's ROE. The higher the level, the greater the expected return on that stock. The more consistent a stock's ROE, then the more accurate will be our overall projections.
3. The price to earnings ratio (P/E) reflects investor expectations about the future earnings of the company, and these expectations rise and fall with the performance of the economy, both actual and perceived.
4. The more consistent the stock in the past, the more comfortable we are with our projections for the future.
5. If we cannot accurately project the future price due to past inconsistency, we cannot discount back to the present to determine a proper purchase price. And in Buffett's world, the purchase price is all-important.
6. The all-important purchase price determines what our total future return will be. Total return equates to price appreciation plus dividends.
7. The modern-day followers of Clean Surplus ROE do not try to determine the value of a company. But they do value the company relative to the total return they themselves require from that company over the next 10 years.

Chapter 15

The Beginning: The Initial Research

The Dow Jones Industrials

T his book wouldn't be even half complete if I didn't go over the
initial research that eventually led to my published doctoral dissertation research, which we will discuss in Chapter 16. We will
test the Dow Jones Industrial Average in this chapter and then test the
S&P 500, which was the research for the doctoral dissertation. Let's see
if we can use Clean Surplus as was originally intended by the founding
fathers of Clean Surplus Accounting.

I mentioned in the Introduction that I once attended a lecture
(1995) in which a form of Clean Surplus was used as a stock selection
method. I ran home and sat in front of my computer for the next four-
and–a–half months formulating spreadsheets on the Dow 30 stocks. Of
course, at the time I didn't know this method was called Clean Surplus

Accounting and neither did the lecturer. I gathered the necessary data from the Dow 30 stocks for the period 1982 to 1995. The questions I wanted answered were very simple:

1. Do stocks with a high return on equity (ROE) as configured by Clean Surplus Accounting outperform stocks with low ROEs?
2. Could I construct a portfolio of stocks from the Dow 30 Industrials, which would outperform the Dow 30 Industrial Average?

Why Work with the Dow 30?

You are all asking why I chose the Dow Jones 30 Industrials from which to select stocks when most money managers use the S&P 500 as a benchmark for performance. The reason is very simple. The Dow 30 is comprised of 30 stocks, and the S&P 500 is comprised of 500 stocks. Let's see: Research 30 stocks or 500 stocks? I decided to begin with 30 stocks.

Another question arises as to whether money managers should benchmark their results against the Dow or the S&P 500? Most managers question how 30 stocks could possibly represent the entire universe of stocks and just naturally figure that 500 stocks would better represent "the market."

If you go to an on-line service such as bigcharts.com and play around a bit, you can overlay the performance of the S&P 500 against the Dow. As you can see, over time they match one another pretty closely.

This is a good time to bring on a saying that Yogi Berra conjured up one day. I'm just kidding! Warren Buffett is believed to have said the following: It is better to be approximately right than precisely wrong. Notice I didn't use quotation marks because I could be only approximately correct as to who said it first and exactly what was said.

The answer to the question is that we'll use either market average as long as we can beat either average. If we outperform one, we will outperform the other over time.

> Time series analysis uses comparisons over several time periods.

I achieved such great results with the tests on the Dow that I eventually continued on and tested the S&P 500 stocks as well. Chapter 16 will cover the extensive research on the S&P 500 that was used in my doctoral dissertation.

> Cross-sectional analysis uses comparisons during the same time period.

Constructing the Portfolio:
My First Research into Clean Surplus

My original work began in 1995. That year, I began gathering data from 1982 on the Dow 30 in order to obtain several years of numbers with which to construct the Clean Surplus ROE of each Dow stock over a period of time.

Please remember that with Clean Surplus you are developing a book value (owners' equity) different from the traditional accounting book value. But as a starting point in your calculations, you begin with accounting book value for the first year since it is all we have. As you proceed with developing the ROE year after year, you are cleaning up the "dirty" book value. Thus, you would like several years of ROE *before* you begin with your stock selection process. With this first work, I used accounting book value from the beginning of 1982, and cleaned the accounting book value up over the next several years until 1987 when I began the stock selection based on Clean Surplus ROE.

If you analyze data over several time periods, you are using a method known as "time series analysis." By contrast, comparing something today to something else today is called "cross-sectional analysis."

Methodology

Methodology is simply the method or methods (parameters, rules) used for data gathering and data analysis.

For this initial work, I used cross-sectional analysis. I wanted to compare the ROE of each of the Dow 30 stocks one year at a time beginning in 1987.

> ### THE POWER OF ROE
> Please be aware that throughout this book, we discuss the consistency of ROE over many time periods. However, this first work deals with just a single year's comparison.

I initiated my back-testing for the stock selection process beginning with the year of 1987 by selecting eight stocks from the Dow, with the highest 1986 ROEs as configured by the Clean Surplus Accounting method (Figure 15.1). These eight stocks would make up my portfolio for the entire year of 1987.

I did this for each year thereafter. I calculated the 1986 ROEs of all 30 stocks on January 1, 1987. These stocks were then selected for the first portfolio, beginning the first trading day of January of 1987.

Why did I select eight stocks? Well, eight stocks comprised a bit over 25 percent of the Dow 30 stocks. Also, in my first year of selection (1986 ROE for 1987 portfolio), there was a large gap in ROE between the eighth and ninth stock. Thus, a division between the eighth and ninth stocks seemed a good beginning parameter.

I began stock return calculations for 1987 based on 1986 ROE for several reasons. The first reason was I only had access to data beginning in 1982, and I needed several years to clean up the traditional accounting book value. Thus, beginning 1982 through the end of 1986 gave me approximately five years in order to clean up my book value.

Please be aware that fourth quarter results are not available on January 1. Thus, fourth quarter results are estimates. But those estimates for the large cap stocks are fairly accurate.

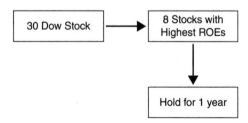

Figure 15.1 1987 Clean Surplus Portfolio

1987: The Year of the Anomaly

Another reason I began forming my portfolio in 1987 was that I wanted to include the market crash of 1987. 1987 was definitely a year of an anomaly because on Monday, October 19, 1987, the Dow fell 22 percent. This day is now infamous and known in history as Black Monday.

A 22 percent decline in one day is certainly out of the ordinary. And it certainly doesn't adhere to an efficient market.

But the term "anomaly" is an academic word meaning you have no clue as to what happened or why it happened. Actually, it's something you can't explain. Ok, like very much out of the normal. Here's an easy way to remember the meaning of anomaly.

Remember that one Star Trek adventure when Captain Kirk and Spock were tooling around the universe and came upon a huge cloud of space stuff? The space stuff was more than just a cloud; it was a living thing. Do you remember what they called it? Since they had no name for a living space cloud, they called it the "Anomaly."

For those of you who didn't see that particular episode, our heroes made friends with the cloud and went on to make many, many more adventures. And now, beam us back to earth, Scotty.

Buffett the Anomaly

The academic world calls Warren Buffett an anomaly because he doesn't fit into the academic theory of the efficient market hypothesis. No one is supposed to outperform the market over time, but indeed Buffett has. Since he doesn't fit into what is supposed to be, he is an anomaly. So when I ran into the office of the head of finance at the university where I taught at the time and I shouted out something like, "Warren Buffett rocks," well, with just a wave of his all-knowing department head hand, he condescendingly dismissed me by saying Buffett is merely an anomaly.

Like, oh yes, that certainly explains it! Is that how I'm supposed to describe Warren Buffett, the god of investing, to my students? Just dismiss whatever doesn't fit into the academic world as merely an anomaly?

Sorry, I got carried away, but I get emotional when people insinuate that Warren Buffett is just "merely" lucky. Ok, back to our work and Clean Surplus Accounting.

More Parameters: The Simple Rules

The other parameters of this research were pretty simple. Each year on January 1, I would calculate the ROEs of all 30 Dow stocks for the previous year. I would then select the eight Dow Stocks with the highest previous year's ROE for my portfolio for the coming year. Remember, this is cross-sectional analysis.

The strategy was to hold those stocks for the entire year. This meant no selling just before market crashes or corrections and no buying at market bottoms. After all, this is research and not marketing.

The only time I could change stocks was on the first trading day in January, and all stocks chosen had to be held for the entire year until the first trading day of the next year.

Just a side note here: If you have a New Year's hangover, the compilations will take you about two hours. If you awake fresh and ready to go, this work could take you just one hour. If you want to go to the computer program, which you can access through a trial period with the purchase of this book or with a subscription through the website, your working time will take you about two minutes. Well, maybe five minutes.

The Test Period Parameters

The portfolio of eight Dow stocks for any one year was selected by taking the eight Dow stocks with the highest ROEs for the previous year. Fourth quarter of the previous year was comprised of estimated earnings and dividends, as these numbers are not known with absolute certainty until some time in January.

The 1987 portfolio consisted of the eight stocks out of the Dow 30 with the highest ROEs for 1986.

The calculations were performed on the first day of the year. Thus, on January 1 of 1987, the 1986 ROEs were calculated. The eight stocks with the highest ROEs became the 1987 portfolio. All eight stocks were held for the entire year.

The Results

Let's observe the results relative to the S&P 500 index in Table 15.1. Notice I have these results up to the end of 2002. This means I back-tested from 1987 to 1995, but from 1996 to 2002 the portfolio was constructed going forward. The column Dow Top 8 shows our selected portfolio for each year.

In this 16-year time frame, the S&P 500 index outperformed the eight-stock portfolio just three times in 1993, 1998, and 1999. Over the 16-year time frame, our eight-stock portfolio returned an average of 18.7 percent with just one negative year, while the S&P returned just 12.4 percent, having negative performances in four years.

Notice that the eight-stock portfolio returned on average 51 percent more per year than the S&P 500. We obtain this statistic by taking the above-average return per year of the top eight stocks (12.4 percent) and dividing it into the average return of the S&P (6.4 percent): 6.4% / 12.4% = 51.6%.

Table 15.1   Results Relative to S&P 500

Years	Year	Dow Top 8	S&P 500	Returns Greater than S&P 500
16	2002	−18.1%	−22.4%	4.3%
15	2001	2.6%	−12.5%	15.1%
14	2000	1.2%	−9.0%	10.2%
13	1999	19.0%	21.0%	−2.1%
12	1998	27.8%	28.7%	−0.9%
11	1997	41.0%	33.4%	7.7%
10	1996	26.9%	23.0%	4.0%
9	1995	50.3%	37.5%	12.8%
8	1994	5.2%	1.3%	3.8%
7	1993	5.5%	10.1%	−4.6%
6	1992	11.9%	7.6%	4.3%
5	1991	43.9%	30.5%	13.5%
4	1990	5.3%	−3.1%	8.4%
3	1989	42.5%	31.7%	10.8%
2	1988	16.7%	16.4%	0.3%
1	1987	18.2%	3.6%	14.6%
Average Returns		**TOP 8**	**S&P 500**	
18.7%		**12.4%**	**6.4%**	

Here's a very interesting point: Over the three horrible years of 2000, 2001, and 2002, the eight-stock portfolio lost 14.3 percent while the S&P 500 lost 43.9 percent. This means that the eight-stock portfolio made more in most good years and lost less in bad years. So if you are in the stock market for the long term, you now know a very good stock selection strategy. More in the next chapter for you nonbelievers.

Compounded Returns

An analysis of returns just wouldn't be complete if we didn't show a chart of how an initial investment of $100,000 would look with the previous returns, so here we are (Table 15.2). Please be aware we are not allowing for any possible income tax consequences.

Reading from bottom to the top, we can see that the Dow Top 8 stocks would have made an awful lot of money: almost 150 percent more than investing in the S&P 500. Please keep in mind that these eight stocks are part of the Dow 30, and because they are in the Dow,

Table 15.2   Compounded Returns

Years	Year	S&P 500	Dow Top 8
16	2002	**$522,651**	**$1,286,085**
15	2001	$673,259	$1,570,311
14	2000	$769,175	$1,530,518
13	1999	$845,619	$1,513,117
12	1998	$698,628	$1,271,848
11	1997	$543,003	$995,108
10	1996	$407,201	$705,750
9	1995	$331,193	$556,015
8	1994	$240,797	$369,888
7	1993	$237,660	$351,738
6	1992	$215,937	$333,401
5	1991	$200,648	$297,919
4	1990	$153,777	$206,989
3	1989	$158,729	$196,589
2	1988	$129,532	$137,928
1	1987	$103,550	$118,150
Beginning Amt.		$100,000	$100,000

they are also part of the S&P 500 index. As we can see, they are among the best-performing stocks in our investing universe if our universe is the S&P 500.

This little exercise shows that stocks with high ROEs are certainly rewarded by the stock market participants. This little exercise shows that people who are able to select stocks with high Clean Surplus ROEs should be rewarded very nicely, thank you.

Stocks with high Clean Surplus ROEs perform better on average than stocks with low Clean Surplus ROEs.

Why do stocks with high ROEs perform better, on average, than stocks with low ROEs? The answer is simple if you think about it for a moment. Stocks with high ROEs are making more of a profit than stocks with low ROEs. Again, think of the difference between a bank paying you 10 percent per year and a bank paying you 20 percent per year. Yes folks, a company that is making more money and reinvesting that money back into itself will be worth more in the future than a company making less money and thus having less money with which to reinvest back into itself.

Is There a Correlation Between the ROEs and the Returns?

There are a lot of systems which when back-tested seem to outperform the averages. Why are our results meaningful?

When you perform research, you are not only obtaining results either positive or negative, but you are searching for a *reason* that you are obtaining those results. And this reasoning is the answer to all our questions.

During this 16-year time frame, the S&P 500 stocks had an average ROE of about 14 percent, while the eight-stock Dow portfolio had an average ROE close to 22 percent. The yearly average return of the S&P during this time was 12.4 percent, and the average return of the eight-stock portfolio was 18.7 percent (Table 15.3).

Table 15.3   Comparisons between S&P and Eight-
Stock Dow

	ROE	Total Return
8-Stock Portfolio	22%	18.7%
S&P 500	14%	12.4%

In other words, the ROEs of both the S&P 500 and the eight-stock portfolio had a strong correlation to the total returns of each of the portfolios.

Once I realized there was a correlation between the ROE and total future returns, a multitude of questions came into my head.

Is it possible to merely look at the ROE (Clean Surplus Accounting) of a portfolio and conclude that the ROE is an indicator of future returns? In other words, would a portfolio with an ROE of 20 percent earn a total return of approximately 20 percent per year in the future? Would a portfolio with an ROE of 20 percent return more than a portfolio of stocks that averaged a 10 percent ROE? And finally, would this system work on portfolios of stocks other than the Dow stocks?

My later doctoral dissertation research on the S&P 500 would answer these questions, but at the time I worked on the Dow stocks, I wasn't even thinking about a dissertation. Remember that in 1995 I was already "old" and I was in the fourth year of a one-and-a-half year master's degree program.

Back to the real question: *Is there a correlation between the ROE and the future returns of a portfolio?* In other words, does the ROE as configured by Clean Surplus Accounting show predictability as was intended by the founding fathers of Clean Surplus Accounting?

During the time frame of 1987 through 2001, there was a very high correlation between Clean Surplus ROE and total returns of both our Top 8 stock portfolio and the S&P 500 stock portfolio.

Note 1: Please don't confuse the ROE of a stock or of a portfolio with the total returns. Clean Surplus ROE is a comparable efficiency ratio, and total return is comprised of price appreciation plus dividends.

Note 2: The ROE of a portfolio is the average ROE of all the stocks making up that portfolio.

Getting Published in an Academic Journal

As I mentioned earlier, it took four-and-a-half months to calculate my work on the Dow 30 just from the years of 1987 through 1995. I added the later years, yes, later. I wrote a research article describing my results for a financial journal and guess what words of wisdom were sent back to me?

They said something like, well, this is nice, but you really should perform your calculations using the 500 stocks in the S&P 500 index.

Folks, my heart was broken. I saw my life flash in front of me. I may really have come upon something fantastic, and I wanted the entire world to know about it, but the academic community didn't want any part of it, at least not in the form I was communicating to them. But I felt the research work must go on, and somehow I must tell the world that there is indeed a measure of predictability in Clean Surplus Accounting. The next several chapters will tell us more. Much more!

SUMMARY

1. Time series analysis is a comparison of data over several time periods.
2. Cross-sectional analysis is a comparison of data during the same time period.
3. A portfolio of eight stocks selected from the Dow 30 using high ROEs as configured by Clean Surplus Accounting was able to more than double the dollar returns of the S&P 500 average over our 16-year test period.
4. During the time frame of 1987 through 2002, there was a very high correlation between Clean Surplus ROE and the total returns of both the Top 8 portfolio and also the S&P 500 index portfolio.

Chapter 16

Continuing Research: The Doctoral Research on the S&P 500

A t the beginning of the doctoral program, the folks running the institutions of higher education tell all the students to begin thinking about the subject of their dissertation. We call it the "big D." It's not divorce, and it's not Dallas; it's the horrible thought of several more years of research. It's the really, really "BIG D."

Just to bring you up to date on the academic parameters, a doctoral program or a Ph.D. program is all about research. As I mentioned in the introduction, the difference between a Ph.D. degree and a doctoral degree is that the Ph.D. develops the theory and the doctor with a doctoral degree tries to put that theory into practical use. Just to confuse things, both these academic designations carry the title of "Doctor." The Ph.D. is just a bit more of a theoretical degree.

Some universities would rather not have doctors with doctoral degrees teaching their students. They would rather employ teachers that
have the Ph.D. designation. I once had an instructor tell me that the
university was in existence to teach the theoretical. Anything practical
should be taught in technical schools. Oh yes, I was as shocked as those
of you reading this.

Please don't forget that I began my doctoral education rather late in
life. I went to a school where most of the students were middle-aged, with
half of them coming from the teaching profession and the other half coming from industry. Those coming from the business world were mostly
successful people in business who wanted the Holy Grail of degrees and
to also learn some theory they could possibly put to practical use.

Why did I just tell you all this? I wanted to write my dissertation
on a subject that I could use in real life and not just any subject to make
my professors happy. I really wanted to take the theory, apply it, and
construct a better portfolio for myself. Or to put it another way, use my
education in order to make money. I guess I'm just a selfish, capitalistic
individual.

The dissertation is a very large research paper usually completed
after all the doctoral coursework is completed. The dissertation is several
hundred pages of research along with many, many pages of supporting
documentation. It is based on existing research work, and the job of the
Ph.D. or doctoral candidate is to add to that body of knowledge.

My problem was I didn't know of any research performed on the
method I had come into contact with through that seminar I once
attended. Thus, I couldn't add to the body of knowledge that possibly
didn't exist. I didn't even know the name of the method, which meant I
couldn't even begin my search.

Finally, a Lead for Clean Surplus Accounting—Buffett, Graham, Ohlson

I know I talked about the following in the Introduction, but many of
you probably didn't read the Introduction, so I think it is worth men-
tioning once again. By the way, the Introduction is a pretty good sea
story in its own right.

I investigated the published research archives for about a year-and-a-half and finally found some information on the "phantom" method I came into contact with through that seminar I had once attended. It was called Clean Surplus Accounting and, folks, I am being totally speculative on the following.

A paper was published in 1989 by James Ohlson on how the Clean Surplus relation could be used in security valuation. Ohlson wrote his paper while at Columbia University. Does anyone remember where Warren Buffett went to school for his master's degree? And does anyone remember whom he studied under while getting his master's degree? Warren Buffett went to Columbia University and studied under Benjamin Graham, who is known as the "Father of Security Analysis."

Again, I'm not implying anything here, but the three of these gentlemen gracing the academic halls of the same school certainly makes for good cocktail party conversation.

The Results of the Research

The following is an excerpt of an article I wrote regarding the test results of a section of my dissertation work:

The purpose of this test is to determine if portfolios constructed using a high average return on equity (ROE) configured using Clean Surplus Accounting are able to outperform the S&P 500 Index.

> The purpose of this test is to determine if portfolios constructed using a high average ROE configured using Clean Surplus Accounting are able to outperform the S&P 500 Index.

Methodology

As I said in the last chapter, methodology is a neat word, which summarizes the rules, framework, parameters, or system(s) set in place before the testing begins. Here are the rules for the research on Clean Surplus ROE and the S&P 500: Yes, *Beyond Buffett*.

1. A spreadsheet was developed for each security used in this test, such as the spreadsheet for Tupperware (TUP) in Table 16.1. The yearly net income (earnings before extraordinary write-offs and future liabilities) and dividends were used in order to obtain Clean Surplus book value (owners' equity).

Note: These numbers are very difficult to obtain during any current period. Thus, the data I have going back to 1982 is very probably the only early data in existence at the present time. This data, along with continuing data, form the basis of calculations for the computer program.

2. The securities used began with the S&P 500 as of December 1982. This list was narrowed due to several limitations. Securities not included in the sample consist of any security that did not include data for the entire sample period of 1982 through 1998. Any companies that merged or were dropped from the index were eliminated from the sample. The final sample consisted of 351 securities.

Notice Tupperware is not calculated in Tables 16.1 and 16.2 for the initial test periods, as I'm just using Tupperware as an example.

3. For the first test period, an eight-year time series average of the ROE of each stock was calculated using the Clean Surplus Accounting method, beginning in 1982 and continuing through 1989.

With Tupperware in Table 16.2, you will see the eight-year average ROE to be 32.7 percent.

Table 16.1   Tupperware (TUP) 3.3%

Year	Owners' Equity	Net Income	Dividends Paid	Return on Equity
2015	$21.32	$6.10	$3.00	28.6%
2014	$18.84	$5.20	$2.72	27.6%
2013	$16.15	$5.17	$2.48	32.0%
2012	$14.17	$3.42	$1.44	24.1%
2011	$11.82	$3.55	$1.20	30.0%
2010	$9.29	$3.53	$1.00	38.0%
2009	$7.45	$2.75	$0.91	36.9%
2008	$5.77	$2.56	$0.88	44.4%

Table 16.2   Tupperware (TUP) 3.3%

Year	Owners' Equity	Net Income	Dividends Paid	Return on Equity
2015	$21.32	$6.10	$3.00	28.6%
2014	$18.84	$5.20	$2.72	27.6%
2013	$16.15	$5.17	$2.48	32.0%
2012	$14.17	$3.42	$1.44	24.1%
2011	$11.82	$3.55	$1.20	30.0%
2010	$9.29	$3.53	$1.00	38.0%
2009	$7.45	$2.75	$0.91	36.9%
2008	$5.77	$2.56	$0.88	44.4%
			8 Year Average ROE	**32.7%**

4. The total return calculations (price appreciation plus dividends) of each stock were calculated over the following four years. Thus, we obtained an eight-year average ROE, and we are trying to see if this average ROE has any bearing on the following four years of total returns (price appreciation plus dividends).

Note: The four-year returns began with the last day of March in order to fully incorporate into the price all earnings announcements for the previous year's fourth quarter. All fourth quarter earnings results are announced by the end of the following first quarter, with most of the announcements occurring during January of the first quarter. Thus, all announcements are fully incorporated into security value by the end of the first quarter of the year.

5. For the second test period, an eight-year period of average ROEs was calculated from 1986 through the end of 1993, followed by a four-year period of total returns (price appreciation plus dividends), beginning the end of March 1994 through end of March 1998.

Notice the Difference

In the following S&P 500 tests, I used an average ROE over eight years to try and predict the average yearly total return (price appreciation plus dividends) over the following four years. With the Dow tests of the previous chapter, I used a one-year ROE to select a portfolio that would outperform the Dow averages over the following one year.

Does an eight-year ROE have any predictive ability over the following four years?

FIRST TEST PERIOD

Average ROE of the eight-year period 1982–1989, followed by average yearly returns (price appreciation plus dividends) over the following four years, from the end of March 1990 to the end of March 1994

SECOND TEST PERIOD

Average ROE of the eight-year period 1986–1993, followed by average yearly returns (price appreciation plus dividends) over the following four years, from the end of March 1994 to the end of March 1998

Standardized Against the Market

The term "market returns" is meant to be the returns of the S&P 500 for the purposes of this study. The average ROE of all the S&P stocks in the study becomes the market ROE.

Portfolio Construction

1. The 351 securities were sorted in descending order of each stock's eight-year average ROEs for the first period of 1982–1989. Portfolios consisting of 10 stocks each were selected, beginning with the 10 stocks exhibiting the 10 highest average ROEs. The second portfolio consisted of the stocks with the next 10 highest ROEs. The average ROE of each 10-stock portfolio was used as a predictor against the total return of each portfolio for the subsequent four years of 1990–1994.

2. A second selection of portfolios chosen in the same manner was used with average ROEs of the eight-year period of 1986 through 1993

as a predictor of total returns for the period from the end of March 1994 through end of March 1998.

> The first portfolio consists of the 10 stocks with the highest eight-year average ROE. The second portfolio consists of the 10 stocks with the next highest ROEs.

3. All stocks and portfolios were adjusted for risk. Risk was determined by beta (the most widely accepted measure of investment risk) obtained from Value Line. Total returns were divided by beta to obtain risk-adjusted returns.

Note: Beware of your source for beta. Beta will be different depending upon the period of measurement and duration of the periods. A source measuring stock results weekly over a five-year period will be different than measuring stock results monthly over the same five-year period.

The main purpose of this research is to determine if portfolios constructed with stocks of above-average ROEs as calculated by the Clean Surplus Method can outperform the S&P 500 Index.

Results: First Test Period

Table 16.3 shows the portfolio results of the first test period. These results include 14 portfolios, all of which had an average portfolio ROE greater than the average ROE of all the S&P 500 stocks in the test. In other words, they are portfolios with above-average ROEs.

Each portfolio's average ROE (the average of the ROEs of the stocks in each portfolio) from 1982 through 1989 is followed by the risk-adjusted average per year return of end of March 1990 through end of March 1994.

The S&P returned an average of 10.35 percent per year during this time frame. Every one of the portfolios with above-average ROEs outperformed the S&P 500.

Table 16.3   First Test Period Results

10-Stock Portfolio	8 Yr. Avg. ROE 1982–1989	Avg. Yearly Risk-Adjusted Returns 3/31/90–3/31/94	Returns Above S&P
S&P 500		10.35%	
1	53.5%	26.1%	15.8%
2	31.9%	13.7%	3.4%
3	27.0%	15.9%	5.5%
4	24.6%	26.9%	16.5%
5	22.5%	16.4%	6.1%
6	21.4%	18.0%	7.7%
7	20.7%	18.3%	7.9%
8	20.0%	14.6%	4.2%
9	19.6%	26.2%	15.9%
10	19.9%	16.9%	6.5%
11	18.4%	17.6%	7.3%
12	17.8%	23.5%	13.1%
13	17.3%	25.8%	15.5%
14	16.4%	20.6%	10.3%

Results: Second Test Period

The results of the second test period are shown in Table 16.4. Each portfolio's average ROE from 1986 through 1993 is followed by the risk-adjusted average per year return of end of March 1994 through end of March 1998.

The S&P returned 28.7 percent per year during this time frame. Every portfolio that had an average ROE above the total average portfolio ROE outperformed the S&P 500.

Bias

There may be a survivorship bias. Many portfolios outperformed the S&P during the test periods. However, 500 stocks (the entire index) began in 1982, but just 351 securities survived the entire test period. It may be assumed that the securities that did not survive the entire test period were laggard performers, which, of course, is probably why many (if not all) of them are not in the index today.

Table 16.4   Second Test Period Results

10-Stock Portfolio	8 Yr. Avg. ROE 1986–1993	Avg. Yearly Risk-Adjusted Returns 3/31/94–3/31/98	Returns Above S&P
	S&P 500	28.7%	
1	39.9%	39.0%	10.4%
2	31.3%	37.8%	9.1%
3	27.0%	49.5%	20.8%
4	23.9%	37.7%	9.0%
5	21.9%	31.9%	3.2%
6	20.8%	51.5%	22.9%
7	20.1%	45.4%	16.8%
8	19.4%	55.1%	26.4%
9	18.9%	36.8%	8.1%
10	18.3%	34.2%	5.6%
11	17.6%	33.3%	4.6%
12	16.7%	36.9%	8.2%
13	16.1%	42.5%	13.9%
14	15.4%	33.1%	4.4%

Large Cap Bias

The S&P 500 is primarily a large cap (large capitalization) index. Thus, we cannot be certain that this strategy works well with smaller issues or stocks with less than an eight-year history of earnings.

Summary of Results

This initial work shows that the level of portfolio ROE with owners' equity configured by Clean Surplus Accounting does indeed have a direct relation to the level of future total returns.

The portfolios selected from the S&P 500 with higher average ROEs than the average portfolio did indeed outperform the market averages. In these test periods, all portfolios with above-average ROEs as configured by Clean Surplus Accounting *outperformed* the S&P 500 Index.

I don't know about you, but these tests show some pretty interesting results relative to predictability. These results show that the system works in average markets (first test period) and super bull markets, as in the second test period.

The Dow research in Chapter 15 (especially years 2000, 2001, and 2002) indicates that the predictability of better performance also holds true in horrible markets. Not that the stocks always have positive returns, but in our research, the returns of portfolios with higher than average ROE stocks (Clean Surplus) do better than portfolios of stocks with lower than average ROEs when the ROEs are configured by the Clean Surplus method.

Note: Only portfolios with higher than average ROEs are shown in this chapter.

> The research shows that the ROE as configured by Clean Surplus Accounting does have a direct correlation to the total returns of portfolios over two four-year periods.

Other Work

Work was also performed with portfolios of 30 stocks each (Figures 16.1 and 16.2). The results for the larger portfolios (30 stocks) were even

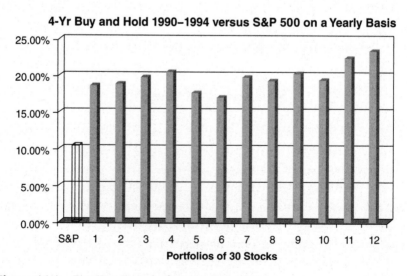

Figure 16.1   First Test Period of 30-Stock Portfolios

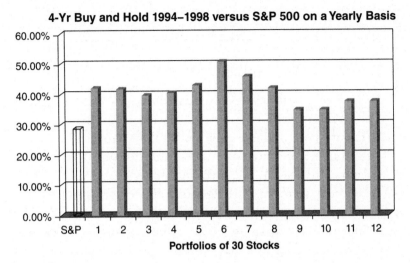

4-Yr Buy and Hold 1994–1998 versus S&P 500 on a Yearly Basis

Figure 16.2   Second Test Period of 30-Stock Portfolios

more predictable and much more consistent than with the portfolios of 10 securities. For the statisticians reading this, the tests on larger portfolios of 30 securities showed a 79–80 percent correlation of portfolio ROEs and future total returns.

1. The first 30-stock portfolio was formed by combining the first three 10-stock portfolios. The second 30-stock portfolio was formed by combining the next three 10-stock portfolios and so on.
2. The average return of the S&P 500 index over each four-year period is shown on the left in Figures 16.1 and 16.2.
3. All of the 30-stock portfolios with above-average (above the S&P ROE) ROEs are shown to the right of the S&P and numbered 1 to 12.

> The research work shows that portfolios of 30 securities exhibit greater predictability than portfolios constructed of 10 securities, when predictability of total returns (stock appreciation plus dividends) is correlated to ROE as configured by Clean Surplus Accounting.

SUMMARY

1. Time series analysis is comparison of data over several time periods.

2. Cross-sectional analysis is comparison of data during the same time period.

3. The purpose of the tests on the S&P 500 stocks was to determine if portfolios constructed, using a high average ROE with equity (book value) configured by Clean Surplus Accounting, were able to outperform the S&P 500 Index.

4. This research shows that the ROE as configured by Clean Surplus Accounting does have a direct, positive correlation with the total returns of portfolios over two four-year time periods.

5. The research shows that portfolios of 30 securities exhibit greater predictability than portfolios constructed of 10 securities, when predictability is correlated to ROE as configured by Clean Surplus Accounting.

6. During these test periods, all portfolios with ROEs greater than the average ROE of the S&P 500 stocks outperformed the S&P 500 relative to total returns. I said, *all portfolios.*

Chapter 17

Rules for Structuring a Great Growth Portfolio

This is a very short chapter because the rules for structuring a portfolio are very simple and straightforward. You've learned a lot over the past chapters and in order to go forward, you need to know what you are looking for which in turn will help you better understand the following chapters.

Here are the simple rules.

1. Choose stocks with Clean Surplus returns on equity (ROEs) above 20 percent.
2. We want stocks that have a good history of operation. Buffett likes to see a 10-year history. But there are some stocks out there that have less of an operating history, but have high and rising ROEs.
3. Choose stocks with low or no dividends. After all, this is a growth portfolio. Don't worry, we have a place for those high dividend stocks in our Dividend Income and Growth portfolio.

4. We want stocks with little debt. I will discuss this in this chapter.

5. Stocks with rising ROEs are wonderful stocks even if the stock has a Clean Surplus ROE below 20 percent.

6. Sell a stock when the Clean Surplus ROE drops below 20 percent.

That's it! Yes, those are the rules, but let's discuss them a bit further.

As you are now aware, selecting stocks is easy, but finding the past and even present information is difficult, which is why we have a computer program. Since we have a computer program, let's use it. By the way, the computer program is as easy as the rules just listed.

For my doctoral dissertation research, I used the stocks out of the S&P 500 index. Every now and then, there will be an up and coming stock that is not in the S&P or may be in another index, which is why we have more than 1,800 stocks in our database.

To find stocks with an ROE above 20 percent we simply go to the computer program and click on any of the headings, and the computer program will sort all 1,800 stocks in both ascending and descending order of their ROEs. Simple as that.

Table 17.1 is a sample with stocks sorted by the 2014 ROE. I think you will recognize most of these names.

We would like to select stocks that have a 10-year operating history. We can go across the top from left to right and, looking at Gilead Sciences, we see that it has at least a 10-year operating history above 20 percent for all multiyear periods.

Table 17.1   Stocks Sorted by the 2014 ROE

Company	Sym	2014 ROE	3-YR Avg ROE	5-YR Avg ROE	10-YR Avg ROE	Div	Debt (years)
Gilead Sciences Inc.	GILD	53%	33%	32%	40%	0%	1
Philip Morris International Inc.	PM	43%	50%	60%	N/A	4%	3.4
The Priceline Group Inc.	PCLN	39%	42%	48%	45%	0%	0.7
Lorillard, Inc.	LO	38%	37%	38%	N/A	4%	2.8
Apple Inc.	AAPL	32%	40%	47%	39%	2%	0.4
BlackRock, Inc.	BLK	31%	32%	33%	32%	2%	2.4

We have a problem with Philip Morris in that Philip Morris changed its name to Altria and then split into two companies. Altria is the U.S. tobacco company, and Philip Morris International is the international tobacco company. Of course, this was due to a host of domestic lawsuits, but the point here is that Philip Morris International does not have a 10-year operating history. Under the 10-year average ROE we see N/A. This means "not applicable," but we know Philip Morris has been around since forever—just not in the form of separate companies. However, Philip Morris has a 4 percent dividend, and we would rather have stocks with small or no dividends as we are forming a growth portfolio. We'll skip Philip Morris for our growth portfolio, but save it for our Dividend Income and Growth portfolio.

Going down one more stock we see Priceline. Look at that nice high ROE. Let's take a closer look at Priceline by clicking on the name, Priceline (Table 17.2).

I first look at the heading Return on Equity. Remember, this is the Clean Surplus ROE. It is declining since 2011, but it is still way above 20 percent. Next I want to look at the dividends. No dividends. I like that.

I want to look next, and this is so important, at the 2008 and 2009 Net Income heading. We see that in those recession years the net income rose, whereas in some cyclical stocks the net income will go down. A rising net income in a recession tells us this is not a cyclical stock. This is a very good thing.

Table 17.2   The Priceline Group Inc. NASDAQ - PCLN

Year	CS Owners' Equity	Net Income	Dividends Paid	Retained Earnings	Return on Equity
2015	$186.61	$65.00	$0.00	$65.00	35%
2014	$134.61	$52.00	$0.00	$52.00	39%
2013	$92.89	$41.72	$0.00	$41.72	45%
2012	$61.61	$31.28	$0.00	$31.28	51%
2011	$38.16	$23.45	$0.00	$23.45	62%
2010	$24.67	$13.49	$0.00	$13.49	55%
2009	$16.12	$8.55	$0.00	$8.55	53%
2008	$10.16	$5.96	$0.00	$5.96	59%
2007	$6.12	$4.04	$0.00	$4.04	66%
2006	$5.19	$0.93	$0.00	$0.93	18%
2005	$4.42	$0.77	$0.00	$0.77	17%
2004	$3.66	$0.76	$0.00	$0.76	21%

Table 17.3 is a very recent example of taking a stock out of our portfolio when the ROE fell below 20 percent. Panera Bread was in our portfolio for a bit over four years. However, at the end of 2013, the forecasted numbers for 2014 showed that the ROE would be declining below 20 percent. You can look at the net income and see that it is still rising, but it is the *rate of increase* that is declining as shown by the decreasing return on equity.

I would like to make one very important point here. Panera is still a good company with a Clean Surplus ROE around 17 percent. Remember that the average stock in the S&P 500 index is approximately 14 percent so going forward and over the longer term, Panera should still outperform the averages. But always remember the bank example. Would you rather put your money in a bank paying you 17 percent or a bank that is paying you 22 percent?

Thus, goodbye Panera and hello to . . . Monster Beverage.

Looking at Table 17.4, we see Monster pays no dividends, which we like in a growth company. The past three years shows an average ROE around 23 percent, which means the net income is growing at a very steady pace.

Table 17.3   Panera Bread Company NASDAQ - PNRA

Year	CS Owners' Equity	Net Income	Dividends Paid	Retained Earnings	Return on Equity
2015	$45.67	$7.70	$0.00	$7.70	16.9%
2014	$38.82	$6.85	$0.00	$6.85	17.6%
2013	$32.14	$6.68	$0.00	$6.68	20.8%
2012	$26.25	$5.89	$0.00	$5.89	22.4%
2011	$21.60	$4.65	$0.00	$4.65	21.5%
2010	$17.98	$3.62	$0.00	$3.62	20.1%

Table 17.4   Monster Beverage Corporation NASDAQ - MNST

Year	CS Owners' Equity	Net Income	Dividends Paid	Retained Earnings	Return on Equity
2015	$12.45	$2.85	$0.00	$2.85	22.9%
2014	$10.05	$2.40	$0.00	$2.40	23.9%
2013	$8.10	$1.95	$0.00	$1.95	24.1%
2012	$6.24	$1.86	$0.00	$1.86	29.8%
2011	$4.71	$1.53	$0.00	$1.53	32.5%
2010	$3.57	$1.14	$0.00	$1.14	31.9%

Here's the good part. In the two years since we made that change, Panera has no gain, while the S&P 500 index has risen 35 percent and Monster Beverage has risen 70 percent.

Now you can see the difference between a nice, high, and steady ROE, and ROE that is declining.

Just one more point: Even though Panera has lost ground over the past year as I write this, we must remember that over five years up to 2015, Panera has gained 200 percent while the S&P has gained approximately 95 percent. However, Monster has gained about 400 percent.

Bottom line is we're replacing a very good stock with a better stock.

Debt

> If a company takes all of its earnings and uses those earnings just to pay off its debt, how many years will it take to pay off all the debt?

I would like to mention debt. Please remember that I teach finance and advanced finance at some of our fine universities. We have models that tell us what the most efficient use of debt should be in a corporation. In other words, if a corporation can borrow money at 10 percent, but make a 12 percent profit on that borrowed money, then the company should borrow money, but only up to a certain point. If a company borrows too much money, it won't be able to borrow at 10 percent any longer. The cost of borrowing will go up as the amount of borrowing increases.

Oh yes, this can get a bit complicated, but Buffett, as usual, has a better way. He asks a simple question: If a company takes all of its earnings and uses it to only pay off its debt, how many years will it take to pay off all the debt? Buffett says that if a company can pay off its debt with earnings within five years, then the company is okay in his book.

Personally, in today's world I like to see a three-year-or-less payback period.

Most computer programs will tell you how much debt a company has in dollar amounts or what the debt to equity ratio is. Our computer

Table 17.5 Panera Bread Company NASDAQ - PNRA

Price	P/E Ratio	Purch. Today	Div.	Debt (yrs)	MCap
157.48	22.4	212.89	0	0	4.3b

Table 17.6 Monster Beverage Corporation NASDAQ - MNST

Price	P/E Ratio	Purch. Today	Div.	Debt (yrs)	MCap
92.38	28.3	87.46	0	0	15.5b

program tells you how many years it will take to pay off the debt if the earnings were used only to pay its debt.

Let's look at Panera once again (Table 17.5). Under Debt (yrs), you see 0. This means Panera has no debt. Let's take a look at Monster Beverage (Table 17.6). We can see that Monster also has no debt. No debt is a good thing.

SUMMARY

This chapter sets down some very easy rules to follow, especially if you use the computer program. Before I had the computer program, I had all the information in the form of Excel spreadsheets. Once I had the spreadsheets set up, which took many of my students about a year, it would take about a day each week to input the data as it became available. We are now to a point where I just turn on the computer and our very able computer guru puts all the information I need at the tip of my fingers.

We have tutorial videos on our website that show the workings of the computer program. As changes are made every now and then, we update the videos. Yes, it's that simple.

Chapter 18

Great, Great Job, but You're Fired

Now that you know the simple rules of structuring a great growth portfolio, let's take a break from the rules and the numbers while I tell you the story of a group of my students who were able to more than double the returns of the market during the bull market years of 1998 and 1999, simply by following the rules you just read about in the previous chapter. They did so well that I was almost fired as their instructor. Why? Because the academic community teaches its students that they cannot outperform the market averages without taking on more risk than the risk of the market. And here was a class of students that were knocking the socks off the professional money managers out there in Investment Land. Those of you from the world of academia will certainly relate to this story.

A New Definition

The definition of "stupid" is when smart people do dumb things. This is my very own definition, and you'll see how it comes into play toward the end of this chapter. The good thing about smart people is they have the ability to realize they are being illogical, and they also have the ability to reverse their periods of insanity, which you will also see later in this chapter.

The Research Begins

I began the doctoral program at a university that was able to differ itself from the mainstay type of school in that you didn't have to be a full-time student in order to enter the program. This school had two time periods in which the courses were taught. One schedule consisted of weekend classes. Yes, full days on Saturday and Sunday. Each class on the weekend schedule lasted several months, with each class meeting one weekend per month. This schedule allowed you ample time to prepare for the next class.

The second schedule consisted of six days in a row of classes. The student attended class from 8 a.m. to 5 p.m. each day and at the end of six days, you were certainly worn out. This schedule had one drawback. You had to do all your preparation work in advance, and if you weren't prepared you couldn't begin the class.

When you signed up for the six-day course, you received a big box in the mail three months before the class. What was in the big box? It included the text or texts for the course, ancillary books that had to be read prior to your first class, and a three-ring binder that was fatter than my 4-foot 9-inch, 240-pound grandmother, who couldn't speak English because she was from the old country. There were also some surprises in the box that consisted of miscellaneous course material that had to be finished prior to class. The binder included instructions for a research paper that had to be sent in to the instructor prior to the beginning of class. The nice thing about this three-month preparation period was we had full access to the instructor via phone and e-mail prior to the beginning of the course.

How long did it take to prepare for the first day of class? About three months, which is why you were sent this big box three months prior to class.

The First Class

My very first class was a finance class. This class was filled with middle-aged folks with half of the folks coming from the teaching profession and the other half coming from the world of business. Folks from the teaching profession were there to obtain the Holy Grail of all degrees, so they could compete for jobs in the academic profession in colleges and universities as heads of departments and deans or associate deans. The degree was needed in order to begin the path to the top of the academic world.

The business folks were already successful in their respective segments of industry and were in this school in order to learn some of the theories of finance that they could take back into the business world in order to put new ideas into practice.

The greatest part of this school is that our instructors were folks that had Ph.D.s or doctorate degrees and were working in the business world. Thus, my instructors had mastered both the academic world and the business world. Yes, we were taught by people who knew both sides.

Barbara

Barbara was one of those gals who immediately garnered attention when she walked into a room. She had blond hair, piercing blue eyes, a type-A personality, all the confidence in the world, and a diamond ring that was heavier than my box full of course material. When guys such as myself are young, we would never, ever dare to even approach a girl such as Barbara. But I was older and much more confident with myself when I saw her, but still was able to muster just a smile and a very quick hello.

One of the items we had to prepare for this class was a 30-minute presentation on the subject we were researching for our dissertation. The presentation had to relate to finance, so some of the students who weren't majoring in finance had a problem right off the bat. Barbara was the first one up to present and her major was definitely *not* finance.

However, she pulled her presentation off so well and set the bar so high that you could smell the fear of the other 15 or so people that had yet to present.

When Barbara was finished, the instructor laughed for several minutes and while still laughing said in his rather thick accent, "Which one of you crows are going to compete with that?" Nobody raised their hand, but I said, "Sir, I think you mean chickens, not crows." He started laughing really hard and said, "OK, Mr. Belmonte, you're up right now, and for being such a wise guy, expand your presentation to one hour. Let's see how well you can think on your feet."

Well, here I was being asked to speak on my favorite subject, which is Clean Surplus and Warren Buffett. I had already come equipped with a PowerPoint presentation on my laptop and going for a full hour was going to be a day at the beach.

I don't want to pat myself on the back, but after my presentation, the bar was now raised higher than the tallest basketball player could jump. My classmates demanded that the presentations should be put on hold until the next day so they could all have more time to prepare.

The class continued for another five days and things went well. The instructor was fantastic and went into detail on some of the theories of several Noble Prize winners: Markowitz's modern portfolio theory, Tobin's separation theory, and Sharp's capital asset pricing model, as well as some theorists most folks never heard of. I had a great time since I knew all about these theories. The instructor and I would go back and forth in friendly fashion and have little discussions regarding portfolio formation. It was one of the best classes I ever took. However, some students, not being finance majors, were ready to jump out of the one-story window.

The next to the last day of class the instructor went over the outline of the four-hour final exam, during which time several folks passed out. Well, not really, we just heard a lot of moans and groans. You see, on the doctoral level of education, final exams are very rare. Usually, the students must prepare a very detailed research paper, but this instructor was different. He wanted a four-hour final exam and that was that, and from what the instructor went over, this exam was going to be unbelievable to say the least.

It was then that Barbara, having formed her elite study group of only her choosing, came over to my work table and with her piercing blue eyes and one hand on her hip asked if I wanted to be in *her* study group.

You folks reading this will recognize this high school tactic of the two groups of people. There was the "in crowd" and there were the rest of us. Just a note here: This behavior goes on until you die, so get used to it. But once you adjust to it, it can be a lot of fun because everyone knows it's a game, including Barbara.

Now I had just one chance to snub the leader of the pack, so I looked at her with a smile and said, "Why, thank you for the invitation, but I really don't intend on studying for the final as a four-hour written exam really shouldn't be all that difficult."

The looks on all their faces were precious. Yes, I did feel sorry for all my new friends, and we all had a great time studying together. Barbara became a dear friend to this day, but this is not what I came here to tell you.

To Teach or Not to Teach?

Landing a teaching job at a University in South Florida is difficult. I know, I know, we all hear about the lack of teachers and the large classes, and so on, but think of it this way. When teachers retire, they all move to South Florida. Armed with a Ph.D. or doctorate degree, they soon get bored with retirement and decide to teach one or two classes per semester just to get out of the house or take a break from the golf course. So, they will take a part-time teaching position for very little money.

Barbara came over to me after the final exam and asked if I thought about teaching while I was getting my doctorate degree? I had taught for a year when I was an engineer and I enjoyed it very much. I graduated from a very prestigious engineering school and had a wonderful opportunity for a career in teaching. Even though I loved the job and the hours, I felt I needed to explore the world.

I looked at Barbara and said that I had thought a little about it, but it was very difficult getting a job. She immediately wrote down three names and three phone numbers at three different universities and said, "Here ya' go. This is for helping me have a good time in finance. If you can do that, then you'll be a great teacher."

I called the three names on Barbara's list, got three interviews, and three job offers. Yes, Barbara knew all the important people in the world of academics, and I found out later that she was very influential.

During my first interview I was asked if I had the credentials to teach international finance. International finance is all about hedging currencies, setting up asset-based lending, options, futures, and currency swaps. I told the dean that I was very familiar with all of the above. He then looked at me square in the eyes (he was a former Marine and I'm sure he used that look with his kids) and asked, "Do you know anything about investing?" Well, that's a "duh" question, as you all know by now, so I looked him square back in the eyes and said, "I certainly do. What are you thinking?"

What he was thinking was starting a new program at his university. It was to be called a Student Managed Investment Program. The actual name was Portfolio Management I and Portfolio Management II. This was going to be fun. I had just begun teaching, and here I was with my own office and head of a separate subdepartment consisting of one person, which, of course, was me.

The students had access to $50,000 of the school's endowment money. My job was to teach them the intricacies of investing. And I did just that. Teaching this class was a great situation. I taught the students about investing, and they did a lot of research for me that became part of my doctoral dissertation. The students were making money for the school's endowment, I was getting research done, which meant I had time to go to the beach (remember the beach factor), and the students were learning things that they could ever learn in any other college or university in the entire world. They were learning how the greatest investor in the world picked stocks for his very famous portfolio, Berkshire Hathaway.

Could things get any better? Highly unlikely, but what I found out was they could be a lot worse.

Sometimes it rains. And sometimes the rain is accompanied by damaging winds and really big hailstones.

One bright day, I was headed to my office as happy as a songbird. This was early 1999, and the market was having a great run. Everybody was happy.

My office was next to the office of the head of the finance department. As I walked by and said hello, he beckoned me into his office. "Joe, the dean wants to see you in his office in half an hour. I can't let you go up there (the dean's office was up in heaven someplace) without telling you the reason for the meeting. The dean doesn't know I'm telling you this, but he and the board want to fire you because your students are making too much money. If they are making too much money, it must mean you are teaching them very risky strategies."

Talk about big hailstones, but I had an advantage. The dean didn't know that I knew the reason for the meeting. I went out to the trunk of my car and got out a very, very thin book called *Research of Clean Surplus Accounting*.

I went up to the dean's office, smiled, and said hello. Before the dean could say anything, I pulled out my little book and said, "Dave, did you ever hear of Warren Buffett?" He nodded in his dean-like manner and said, "Yes of course." I said, "Did you ever hear of Clean Surplus Accounting?" He replied, "No, I have not." I told him that this little book I had in my possession contained the only academic research papers on Clean Surplus Accounting in the entire world. I added that Clean Surplus Accounting was the topic of my dissertation, which had been approved by my dissertation committee. (A dissertation committee consists of four Ph.D.-type folks who must approve each step in the dissertation process. They are NEVER wrong in the eyes of academia). I concluded by saying, "Dave, Clean Surplus is the method used by Warren Buffett, the world's greatest investor. And Clean Surplus research is what I am teaching my students."

Dean Dave looked at his watch and at two of the board members who were also in the room. The dean of the business school then said in his most authoritative voice, "Well, this meeting was scheduled for an hour-and-a-half. I think we're finished so why don't we all go to lunch?" We went to lunch, and I never heard another thing about the students making too much money, and the dean never found out that I knew.

Several Things

The program ended that spring because there was political infighting at that time. Dean Dave was eventually forced out, and the new dean wanted everything that Dean Dave had developed dissolved. This was academia at its worst. However, I will always appreciate and have respect for Dean Dave for being able to recognize that he was wrong and, in a moment, make things right again. That must have been his Marine training. I was happy I was able to finish the two semesters with the students, several of whom went into the field of investing and had and continue to have great careers. All the students were offered jobs after graduation because of this one class.

The school year of the class was fall 1998 and spring 1999. The student's portfolio was up a risk-adjusted return of 62 percent with names like Dell, Microsoft, Oracle, Merck, Intel, Cisco, and Pfizer. Not exactly the high risk that was perceived by the board. The market was up about 20 percent during that time frame. The students kicked butt, tripling the returns of the averages.

SUMMARY

If you go into a meeting, always know more about the folks in that meeting than they know about you.

And yes, you can be fired for doing a great job. Some people will always see you as a threat, but as my wonderful father always said, "They can take everything from you, but they can never take away your education."

Chapter 19

Stocks on Our Radio Show

Back in 2012

Let's have some fun with Clean Surplus. We produced a radio program over a two-and-a-half-year period with which we had more fun than people should have. Listeners would both e-mail and call us regarding stocks they were interested in and ask us to perform our Clean Surplus analysis on their favorites. We kept a log of all these stocks during 2011 in order to see how the Clean Surplus method worked on a random selection of stocks. At the end of the year, we put all the stocks together to see how the stocks performed over the previous five years. I think all of you will be very surprised at the results we found in back-testing our random selection of stocks during this time period.

Please be aware that this chapter is not pure academic research. It is just having fun. What's the difference? Academic research takes a long time to implement, and research must be performed using the rules of academia. One must perform the work of a research scientist, which is the hat I wore when I took three years of my life in order to write and publish my doctoral dissertation on the Clean Surplus method. In order to have academic research published in a meaningful journal, the research must be approved by a group of academics with extreme knowledge of the particular area that the research falls into.

Before continuing on, please remember the goals of Clean Surplus. Clean Surplus is a model developed by the accounting profession, which allows investors to compare and also predict portfolio returns. Comparability and predictability are not available through the use of the traditional accounting statements. Clean Surplus standardizes owners' equity and thus allows us to compare the operating efficiency (return on equity) of one stock to another stock, even across industry lines.

The following work covers all the stocks we analyzed on our daily radio show *Buffett and Beyond* during the entire year of 2011. This report is dynamic in that, as we aired our radio program and researched stocks on a daily basis, we added those stocks to our ongoing list throughout the entire year.

The main question we must ask in our Clean Surplus analysis is, "Do portfolios made up of stocks with higher Clean Surplus return on equity (ROEs) outperform portfolios made up of stocks with lower ROEs?"

> Do portfolios made up of stocks with higher Clean Surplus ROEs outperform portfolios made up of stocks with lower ROEs?

If the answer to this question is "yes" (and it is), then our research has added greatly to the knowledge of the investment world. Our research was originally published in the academic world in the form of my 2002 doctoral dissertation. The published dissertation consisted of statistics that showed that every portfolio, which was predicted to outperform the S&P 500 Index, did so over every four-year period on a risk-adjusted basis for eight consecutive years.

If you compare these results to the professional portfolio managers who manage the publicly registered mutual funds, we find (2002 research report) that, over any 10-year period, 96 percent of these professional portfolio managers are not able to outperform the S&P 500 index. Thus, if the answer to our question is "yes," then the Clean Surplus methodology shows that followers of this Clean Surplus method using our investment parameters are able to outperform 96 percent of the professional money managers who run the publicly registered mutual funds over any 10-year period.

After the publication of the academic doctoral dissertation research, we received approval of our Clean Surplus seminar both by the State of Florida and also by the National Association of State Boards of Accountancy (NASBA). This approval meant that we were approved to teach our course to Certified Public Accountants (CPAs) for their continuing professional education credits. It is very interesting to note that, up to that time and to my knowledge since then, our 10-credit self-study course for CPAs was the only course not written by a CPA that was ever approved by the National Association of State Boards of Accountancy (NASBA). We passed muster because the results of our research were so compelling and because of my credentials relative to research and practical application of that research.

The Structure of This Report

We divided all of our analyzed stocks into three portfolios and compared these portfolios against the S&P 500 index. As you all know by now, the S&P 500 is the most widely used benchmark for the general stock market.

The first portfolio, or group of stocks, consisted of all stocks that had Clean Surplus ROEs of 20 percent or higher. The second portfolio consisted of stocks with ROEs ranging between 14 percent and 19 percent. The final portfolio consisted of all stocks with ROEs less than 14 percent. The average stock in the S&P 500 index has an ROE of approximately 14 percent.

In order for the Clean Surplus methodology to hold true, the first and second portfolios, both with ROEs higher than the S&P 500 index,

Table 19.1 Summary of All Portfolios

	Portfolio ROE	5 Yr Total Returns
Portfolio No. 1: ROEs 20% and higher	29%	**158%**
Portfolio No. 2: ROEs from 19% to 14%	16%	**47%**
S&P 500 Index	14%	**0%**
Portfolio No. 3: ROEs below 14%	9%	**−4%**

should have outperformed the S&P 500 index. The first portfolio should outperform the second one, and both these portfolios should outperform the third one.

As we can see from Table 19.1, Portfolio No. 1, consisting of stocks with average ROEs of 29 percent, outperformed all other portfolios over the five-year period from 12/31/2006 through 12/31/2011. Portfolio No. 2 was the next highest performing portfolio, and Portfolio No. 3 was the lowest performing portfolio of our three portfolios.

Clean Surplus tells us that portfolios with higher Clean Surplus ROEs should outperform portfolios with lower Clean Surplus ROEs.

The most important message to take away from Table 19.1 is that portfolios made up of stocks with higher Clean Surplus ROEs outperform portfolios with lower Clean Surplus ROEs. Thus, if we want to outperform the market averages, we must fill our portfolios with stocks that have higher Clean Surplus ROEs than the average stock in the S&P 500 index. The average stock in the S&P 500 index has an ROE of approximately 14 percent. Thus, we must fill our portfolios with stocks that have ROEs higher than 14 percent.

SUMMARY

I hope you are beginning to understand that there is a much easier method of stock selection than you are all accustomed to. You don't have to spend all your time reading, watching, and listening to all the analysts out there in investment land. All you have to do is know which companies are making the highest and most consistent revenue on invested capital. How do you do this? Why, from the Clean Surplus ROE, of course.

MORE SUMMARY AND VERY IMPORTANT

There was a period of 10 years when the S&P 500 index did not appreciate one bit. You hear about this period all the time when someone on TV is trying to make a point about this or that, depending on what they are trying to sell you.

Our test period in this chapter covered 5 of those 10 years where the S&P index did not appreciate. However, if you selected individual stocks that were growing during that period, you would have done very well indeed.

Always remember that stocks with high Clean Surplus ROEs are those companies that are: first, making a great return on the equity money invested into them; and, second, continuing to earn a great return on all the yearly profits reinvested back into them year after year.

And seriously folks, doesn't it make common sense that these are the companies that you want in your portfolios?

Chapter 20

Stories of Audience Hecklers

I am often asked to present my one- or two-hour seminar in front of CPAs, investment groups, and sophisticated investors.

During 2013 I presented in front of a chapter of the Broward County, Florida American Association of Individual Investors (AAII). It was the first time I introduced my computer program, which was still very much in the testing phase but certainly workable enough to show to my audience.

This seminar was especially noteworthy as one of the members was a retired mutual fund manager from Canada. After my seminar presentation we had our usual question and answer session in which "Mr. Antagonistic" asked the following question. I'm not quoting him, as I don't have his exact wording, but it went something like this: *After all is said and done, what value have you added to the investment profession? I (meaning him) ran several mutual funds and we were very successful so why would we need something like your system of stock selection?*

Now here I am standing in front of about 30 folks who all knew as much about investing as most professionals. They all loved the presentation, as Clean Surplus was opening their eyes to a new, wonderful, and meaningful method of stock selection that they had never been exposed to before. This system was not complicated and made perfect common sense. They were also a little upset by the tone of our self-described "very successful" professional money manager as he sat, smirking at his seemingly unanswerable question. His unforeseen problem was he didn't know he was asking his question to a person who had been told many times after the publication of the first edition of this book that I had indeed made a very meaningful contribution to the world of investing.

My answer was simple and straightforward, but began with a question: "When you ran your family of mutual funds, how many analysts did you have working for you?"

"Over a hundred" came his very quick reply.

I responded even faster: "Well, sir, had you been exposed to this seminar and computer program while you were still involved with your mutual funds, you could have fired all of your analysts except one who could have read my book and had access to my computer program, and you would have done much better for your clients."

Needless to say, the crowd went hysterical. "Mr. Downer's" face was red as the members of the audience came up to shake my hand and buy my book. It turned out to be a wonderful day.

Yes, there are some lessons to be learned here. The first is never be in an antagonistic mood and ask a question to the person you are trying to demean unless you already know the answer. This is because a surprise answer will certainly embarrass you to no end.

The second lesson is never try and "take down" a speaker when you are sitting and they are standing, and they also have complete control of the audience.

The third lesson is you cannot be defensive and learn at the same time. Yes, it's called keeping an open mind.

The Know-It-All Half-Back

No, this is not about sports. When people get tired of the snow and sleet, they pick up and move to Florida. After many years of traveling back up north to visit family and friends, they realize they miss the changing of the seasons but dread the long lines at the airport to get on a very crowded plane. Those who don't fly dread even more that long drive all the way back to the Northeast or the Midwest. The decision is then made to move halfway back to from whence they came, and that in turn brings them to North Carolina where they become known as half-backs.

So there I am in front of a group of "half-backs" in North Carolina who are from the New York and New Jersey area via Florida.

After I gave my presentation, we arrived at the question-and-answer period when a person who evidently had not ever lost his brusque city attitude told me (yes, told me) that the Clean Surplus return on equity (ROE) is nice, but you still have to use the age-old system of analysis in order to properly select a portfolio.

I reminded him that I was presenting research, and the research tells us that our bottom-line number represented by the Clean Surplus ROE is a culmination of all those other ratios, sales, revenue, capital expenditures, taxes, interest payments, operating expenses, income, and so on.

This fellow could not understand that there was something he didn't know about the world of investing. At this point two other audience members shouted out for him to shut up and try and learn something new and wonderful. They actually shouted out something worse, but my publisher won't let me put it in writing.

After all was said and done and some of the folks were helping me secure the equipment, the "half-back" came up to me and apologized. He hung his head a bit and said, "Listen, I'm a combination of a horse and a dog. I'm the horse you can lead to water, but can't get to drink, and the dog you can't teach new tricks."

I heard a few years later that Mr. Half-back subscribed to my computer program under a different name, but will not admit to any of his friends that he uses the Clean Surplus ROE.

SUMMARY

The most important point to learn from these short stories is that no matter what system or systems you use to select your stocks, the Clean Surplus ROE should be your final filter. It's back to the same old story. Would you rather invest in a bank paying you 10 percent or a bank paying you 20 percent? Thinking further, if you reinvest all that you earn in a bank paying you 10 percent, your bank account can only grow on average at a 10 percent rate and no more. If you invest in a bank returning you 20 percent and you reinvest all you earn, over time, your bank account will grow, on average at a 20 percent rate. Folks, it's the same with stocks. The Clean Surplus ROE tells us almost everything we need to know about a stock.

Chapter 21

A Great Dividend Income and Growth Strategy—Part I: The Economic Spectrum of Dividend Stocks

What I'm about to show you in this chapter may possibly turn out to be the best portfolio you have ever envisioned that encompasses both income and growth. From previous chapters, you now understand how Clean Surplus works and how we can structure the best growth portfolios relative to risk and return. Certainly the track record speaks for itself. Nothing, or I should say almost nothing, can outperform a great growth portfolio. However, at some point in life, you will need income from your portfolios. Also, a little less volatility is always nice.

> The three steps for forming the dividend growth strategy are deciphered in this chapter. How to select the best stocks was discussed previously, and the enhanced income methods are discussed in Chapter 24.

How would you like to structure a portfolio with a 10-year time horizon that consists of mostly large cap S&P 500 stocks, has the ability to increase in value 150 percent over a 10-year time period, can pay out dividends (after 10 years) of 8–10 percent per year (on original investment) with another 4 percent of added income, and all the while exhibits less volatility than the overall stock market? Yes, we are talking about a great dividend income and growth strategy, and in this chapter we will show you how to develop such a portfolio.

It seems very difficult to find the individual stocks that fit the criteria for this type of portfolio you say? With the help of our computer program, you can structure this portfolio in three easy steps. Well, maybe four easy steps.

There are many variations on dividend income strategies out there in Investment Land, but we want the very best strategy and we want to select the best stocks using the same "Buffett and Beyond" method as we do for our growth portfolios.

I want to say first and foremost that a good growth strategy will outperform a good dividend strategy hands down over time, every time. The reason you hear so much regarding the dividend strategies is that most people do not know how to select good growth stocks. It seems much easier to just look at the dividends of stocks and pick a handful of stocks that are paying

> If you select income stocks only because of their higher dividends, you are missing two very important aspects of a good income and growth portfolio. You have no clue how fast the dividends are growing, and you also have no clue how much the stock itself will grow over the years ahead.

the highest dividends. If you should use the "highest dividend" strategy, you are missing two very important aspects of a good income and growth portfolio. You have no clue how fast the dividends are growing, and you also have no clue how much the stock itself will grow over the years ahead.

Well folks, we know how to determine both the growth of dividends and also the growth of the stock itself. Yes, it's a lot of work, but along with the use of our computer program, it is now very easy to select a great income and growth portfolio. I'm sure you are now interested, so let's see how we can structure this portfolio ourselves.

Portfolio Parameters

In order to develop a superior performing portfolio, we need to pick up a piece of paper and set down our goals.

> We want to develop a portfolio that in 10 years will have great dividend income potential, returning about 8 percent in dividends and another 4–8 percent in added income on the original invested dollars and also the potential for the portfolio to increase in value 150 over those 10 years.

In other words, we are investing now so that in 10 years or so we will have an income portfolio that we can retire on, leave to our spouses, or leave to the rest of the family in our estate. It is also a great legacy to leave to our favorite charity. But first and foremost, this portfolio should fill OUR needs.

There are more important things in life aside from leaving money to others. There's golf, the beach, the lakeside cabin, and the hammock hung between those two trees on the lawn gracing the backyard in your dream vacation-retirement home. Need I add more to this visualization? Now that I've planted the ultimate goal in your minds, let's continue with the parameters of our strategy, but first, a bit of financial education is in order that will help you understand the dynamics of a company and the reasoning behind the selection of the proper stocks for your portfolio.

The Four Stages of the Business Life Cycle

You all learned the four stages of the business life cycle in school if you took any marketing courses. First there is the start-up stage in which growth is extremely fast. Second there is the consolidation stage in which growth slows down, but is still faster than the general economy. Third comes the maturity stage in which growth slows down to a pace about the same as the growth of the general economy. Finally, the company reaches the decline stage in which the growth rate is slower than the general economy.

Let's begin with the start-up stage. Many folks who "play" the markets look for these small start-up companies once they begin making money, or even before they begin making money, hoping that their chosen company will turn into the next IBM or Apple or Priceline. A very old and wise man once told me that one in 10,000 companies make it to the second stage. Well, that's scary! He was talking about the pink sheets and those penny stocks, which never seem to pay out over time.

If the company gets past that dangerous start-up stage and continues to grow, it then enters the growth stage. It is this stage from which we search for companies for our growth portfolio. Since we are trying to outperform the S&P 500 or the Dow 30 Industrials, we want to find companies that are past the dangerous start-up phase and are firmly entrenched in their chosen market and taking market share away from some of the stodgy older companies that are past their days of innovation.

We would like to see companies that have been in this stage for at least 7 to 10 years and show a high and consistent growth pattern. Consistent growth is what the Clean Surplus return on equity (ROE) can tell us.

Since we're on the subject of the growth stage, we also look for companies that pay small or no dividends at all. We would rather see growth companies put *all* of the money they earn back into the company in order to finance ongoing growth. Once a growth company begins to pay dividends, it usually means they are not finding enough projects to invest in or other smaller companies to acquire. As the growth opportunities dwindle or when the company saturates its target market, a growth company will begin to pay dividends back to the shareholders.

As I write this, companies still in the growth stage are Priceline, which pays no dividends; Starbucks, paying a 1.3 percent dividend; and Apple, paying a 2 percent dividend.

Let' take a look at Priceline, which is presently in our growth portfolio (Table 21.1).

Table 21.1   The Priceline Group Inc. NASDAQ - PCLN

Year	CS Owners' Equity	Net Income	Dividends Paid	Retained Earnings	Return on Equity
2015	$186.61	$65.00	$0.00	$65.00	35%
2014	$134.61	$52.00	$0.00	$52.00	39%
2013	$92.89	$41.72	$0.00	$41.72	45%
2012	$61.61	$31.28	$0.00	$31.28	51%
2011	$38.16	$23.45	$0.00	$23.45	62%
2010	$24.67	$13.49	$0.00	$13.49	55%
2009	$16.12	$8.55	$0.00	$8.55	53%
2008	$10.16	$5.96	$0.00	$5.96	59%

As we can plainly see, Priceline is not paying any dividends at all and is earning an extremely high Clean Surplus return on equity. Priceline is putting all the money it earns (net income) back into the company in order to grow. The declining ROE is telling us that the new money being reinvested back into the company is not making the same return as in earlier years. This probably means competition is coming into their space. However, when we see that the ROE is still above our threshold of 20 percent, we know we have a pretty good growth stock.

The third stage is the maturity stage. This stage begins when the company begins to pay dividends to the shareholders, and the Clean Surplus ROE begins to level out or even decline. When the Clean Surplus ROE begins to decline but remains positive, we know that the earnings are still increasing, but are *increasing at a decreasing rate*. It means the company's growth is beginning to slow down. This is the stage where we will garner the stocks for our dividend and growth strategy. Notice in Table 21.2 that Pepsi has a declining ROE and is paying a very nice 3 percent dividend, and the dividends are increasing: more on this in a moment.

Table 21.2   Pepsico, Inc. NYSE – PEP

Year	CS Owners' Equity	Net Income	Dividends Paid	Retained Earnings	Return on Equity
2015	$34.37	$4.85	$2.62	$2.23	14%
2014	$32.28	$4.60	$2.51	$2.09	14%
2013	$30.15	$4.37	$2.24	$2.13	15%
2012	$28.36	$3.92	$2.13	$1.79	14%
2011	$26.41	$3.98	$2.03	$1.95	15%
2010	$24.39	$3.91	$1.89	$2.02	16%
2009	$22.37	$3.77	$1.75	$2.02	17%
2008	$20.76	$3.21	$1.60	$1.61	16%

Finally, a company will enter the decline stage. This is where the company just cannot continue to compete with the "new kids" on the block. J.C. Penney (see Table 21.3) and Sears are two companies that are now losing money. These companies have been around since forever, but just cannot compete with the likes of Target and WalMart. In fact, Sears may be broken up before I even finish this book.

Table 21.3   J.C. Penney Company. Inc. NYSE – JCP

Year	CS Owners' Equity	Net Income	Dividends Paid	Retained Earnings	Return on Equity
2015	$26.30	−$1.55	$0.00	−$1.55	−6%
2014	$36.40	−$3.00	$7.10	−$10.10	−8%
2013	$42.19	−$5.79	$0.00	−$5.79	−14%
2012	$46.09	−$3.50	$0.40	−$3.90	−8%
2011	$46.19	$0.70	$0.80	−$0.10	2%
2010	$45.40	$1.59	$0.80	$0.79	4%
2009	$45.13	$1.07	$0.80	$0.27	2%
2008	$43.39	$2.54	$0.80	$1.74	6%

No, there is no definitive point between the four stages of development. Coke has an ROE that is declining, but it is still making a ton of money for its shareholders. However, it is paying a 3 percent dividend and putting just 40 percent of its earnings back into the company for growth. We would consider Coke in the mature stage, as growth is slowing and it has nowhere to invest its wonderful cash flow. Thus, it is returning about 60 percent of its cash back to the shareholders in the form of dividends. We like to call a company such as Coke a cash cow; and, yes, it is a mature company.

The Maturity Stage

This is the stage from which we want to select stocks that have been great growth companies in the past, but now their growth is slowing down. However, the earnings continue to increase, and since they cannot use all of their earnings for growth, they will pay an increasing dividend to the shareholder. Think Microsoft, Johnson & Johnson, Home Depot, Philip Morris, and Coke. These companies are still growing at the present time, but are increasing their dividends to the shareholders as they run out of growth opportunities.

Very good examples of mature companies are those we all grew up with such as the ones we just mentioned. Let's add Pepsi to this group as we look at a table of the statistics on this great company (Table 21.4). You can see the dividend rate is 3 percent, and the dividends are increasing each year.

The ROE is presently 14 percent, which is a bit below the average stock in the S&P 500 Index. In fact, over the past five years from the writing of this book, both Pepsi and Coke have underperformed the S&P 500 Index.

I would like to point out the "retention rate," which is the percentage of earnings that the company is putting back into the company in order to grow. The money the company is *not* putting back into the company goes back to the shareholders in the form of a dividend. As we look at companies and see a retention rate of around 50 percent or lower, we know the company is in the mature phase of the business life cycle, as it cannot put all the money it is making back into the company in order to grow. Thus, growth is slowing down.

Table 21.4   Pepsico, Inc. NYSE - PEP 3.0%

Year	Dividends Paid	Return on Equity	Retention Rate
2015	$2.62	14%	46%
2014	$2.51	14%	45%
2013	$2.24	15%	49%
2012	$2.13	14%	46%
2011	$2.03	15%	49%
2010	$1.89	16%	52%
2009	$1.75	17%	54%
2008	$1.60	16%	50%

Prior to 1995 (not shown), Pepsi had an ROE in the mid-20s and would have been a great stock to have in a growth portfolio, and we did. However, after 1995, the ROE began to decline below 20 percent. Why? We can only speculate, but when a company is making a lot of money, it begins to invite competition. Think Coca-Cola and all those other soft drink companies. Then came all those other flavored types of ice teas and various sports drinks. There is a lot of money selling flavored water, and that business is spread around in the form of other companies. Think Monster Beverage, which we spoke about in a previous chapter.

Actually, we don't care why the ROE is falling. It is our job to find those companies with nice high ROEs and put those in our growth portfolio. Coke and Pepsi have not been in our growth portfolio for a very long time. In fact, they have not been in our portfolios for over 20 years. But the question is will they be in our income portfolios? Read on to find the answer to this question.

A company sooner or later will enter the decline stage, which is when the growth slows down to below that of the average company. Let's look at J.C. Penney once again in Table 21.5.

The last year this company made any money was in 2011. Ever since then it has lost money, which in turn causes the ROE to become negative. My work on JCP goes back to 1987 when JCP had a very enviable ROE of 18 percent. We could blame everything on WalMart or Target, but whatever the reason (and remember, we don't care what the reason is), this company is indeed in a stage of decline.

Table 21.5   J.C. Penney Company. Inc. NYSE - JCP

Year	CS Owners' Equity	Net Income	Dividends Paid	Retained Earnings	Return on Equity
2015	$26.30	-$1.55	$0.00	-$1.55	-6%
2014	$36.40	-$3.00	$7.10	-$10.10	-8%
2013	$42.19	-$5.79	$0.00	-$5.79	-14%
2012	$46.09	-$3.50	$0.40	-$3.90	-8%
2011	$46.19	$0.70	$0.80	-$0.10	2%
2010	$45.40	$1.59	$0.80	$0.79	4%
2009	$45.13	$1.07	$0.80	$0.27	2%
2008	$43.39	$2.54	$0.80	$1.74	6%

We can see that they are losing less money in 2015 than in 2014, and some of you might consider this to be a turnaround situation, but remember what Buffett says: "Turnarounds seldom turn." I think Buffett says it all.

SUMMARY

We are able to tell what stage of growth or decline a company is in by looking at the Clean Surplus ROE. As the earnings begin to decrease, the ROE will begin to decline. There is no reason to invest in a company that is in its mature or decline stage if you are trying to construct a growth portfolio. As you can see from the examples in this chapter, it is relatively easy to determine which stocks should be in your portfolio and which stocks should be in somebody else's portfolio.

Chapter 22

A Great Dividend Income and Growth Strategy—Part II: Selecting Stocks That Are Growing Their Dividends for Our Portfolio

T his chapter goes through the steps of selecting the stocks for a wonderful and prosperous growth and income portfolio. I will show you how to construct a great portfolio by hand, but folks, our computer program does all this for you in the blink of an eye.

We always want to remember that we are forming portfolios. If we are looking for a portfolio of stocks that on average is paying a 3.5 percent dividend, we can certainly select stocks with a 2.5 percent dividend or a 4 percent dividend as long as the average dividend return is close to our desired return. Why would we even consider a stock for our portfolio that is paying a 2.5 percent dividend when we want our portfolio to average a 3.5 percent dividend return? The answer is because the stock paying a dividend of 2.5 percent may have a faster dividend growth rate or a faster stock growth rate than our average desired dividend growth rate or average desired stock growth rate. What? I'm confused

Let's take some time and go through some examples. First, let's begin with stocks that have high dividends.

A great dividend stock is Philip Morris. Philip Morris changed its name to Altria (MO) and then divided itself into two companies. Altria (MO) is the U.S. company, and Philip Morris International (PM) sells its products everywhere outside the United States. The reasoning was, of course, due to the litigious and anti–business climate developing here in the United States, but that's a story for another book.

Philip Morris International NYSE PM Div. 4.4%

As of this writing, Philip Morris International is paying a very nice 4.4 percent dividend. I certainly like what I see thus far so let's continue on to our next filter, which is the dividend growth rate.

Our second filter is *growth* of the dividends. We would like to add stocks to our portfolio that are growing their dividends on a yearly basis in the range of high single digits. We would like to see a 7 to 8 percent dividend growth rate.

The key to this exercise is to find data on stocks going back at least seven years or so. We want to put the dividends all in a column so that we may find the yearly rate of change of the dividends. Let's continue with Philip Morris International as shown in Table 22.1.

The column we want to look at first is Dividends Paid, and we can see that from 2009 up to 2015 the dividends have been increasing every year. Well, that's a good start.

The next column to the right is the *yearly* dividend growth rate. We can see this rate has been decreasing, but for both 2014 and 2015, the dividends are increasing by 8.9 percent and 8.7 percent, respectively. That is a very nice growth rate for dividends in anybody's book. Philip Morris has passed the second test of the dividend growth rate.

Table 22.1   Philip Morris International

Year	CS Owners' Equity	Net Income	Dividends Paid	Dividend Growth
2015	$13.06	$5.60	$4.24	8.7%
2014	$11.86	$5.10	$3.90	8.9%
2013	$10.18	$5.26	$3.58	10.5%
2012	$8.25	$5.17	$3.24	14.9%
2011	$6.22	$4.85	$2.82	15.6%
2010	$4.74	$3.92	$2.44	8.9%
2009	$3.74	$3.24	$2.24	124.0%
2008	$1.42	$3.32	$1.00	

Let's take a look at AT&T in Table 22.2, which seems to be in everyone's portfolio (except ours) if they want dividend income. It is paying a nice 5.3 percent dividend, but there's more to the story than meets the eye.

Again we want to look at the Dividends Paid column, and we can see that AT&T has increased their dividends every year in our seven-year history. Again, that's a good start. However, going further, things aren't looking so rosy.

The next column to the right is the yearly dividend growth rate. We can see this rate has been a mere 2+ percent for the past seven years. This 2 percent is way below our desired rate of an 8 percent dividend growth rate. Even with a present dividend of 5.3 percent, AT&T just does not fit the bill for our portfolio.

Table 22.2   AT&T, Inc. NYSE – T Div. 5.3%

Year	CS Owners' Equity	Net Income	Dividends Paid	Dividend Growth
2015	$42.28	$2.80	$1.88	2.2%
2014	$41.52	$2.60	$1.84	2.2%
2013	$40.82	$2.50	$1.80	2.3%
2012	$40.25	$2.33	$1.76	2.3%
2011	$39.77	$2.20	$1.72	2.4%
2010	$39.16	$2.29	$1.68	2.4%
2009	$38.68	$2.12	$1.64	2.5%
2008	$38.12	$2.16	$1.60	12.7%
2007	$36.78	$2.76	$1.42	

> The formula: Using AT&T as an example, to find the dividend
> growth rate we would begin with 2015 dividend ($1.88) and
> subtract the 2014 dividend ($1.84) and then divide by the 2014
> dividend: ($1.88 − $1.84)/1.84 = 2.2 percent

Some of you will be defensive of AT&T and voice the argument that,
since our overall portfolio is starting its dividend at about 3.5 percent,
won't AT&T be paying more than its share of dividends? The answer is
yes for the first several years, but where will the AT&T dividend be in
10 years at a 2.2 percent growth rate? The answer will surprise you. The
dividend will grow to 6.6 percent *after* 10 years (Table 22.3). This 6.4
percent rate will not meet our objective of a dividend return of 8 percent in 10 years. And in the next chapter you will see that AT&T does
not even meet our stock growth rate in price. But wait for that segment.
and you'll see what I mean.

Table 22.3   AT&T, Inc. NYSE - T

Year	Projected Dividends
1	5.4%
2	5.5%
3	5.7%
4	5.8%
5	5.9%
6	6.0%
7	6.2%
8	6.3%
9	6.4%
10	6.6%

Let's look at a stock that is not so evident in its dividend or its dividend growth rate. It's a company that has been around for a long while,
and you all know it from everyday use. It's Tupperware (TUP) shown in
Table 22.4.

Table 22.4 Tupperware (TUP) 3.3%

Year	Dividends Paid	Dividend Growth
2015	$3.00	10%
2014	$2.72	10%
2013	$2.48	72%
2012	$1.44	20%
2011	$1.20	20%
2010	$1.00	10%
2009	$0.91	3%

First we look at the dividend and see that it is 3.3 percent. This is a good start. Next we look at the dividends being paid over the years, and we can see that the dividends are increasing each year, which is another good sign. The next step is to see at what growth rate the dividends are growing, and we can see in the past two years the dividend growth rate has been 10 percent. Yes, now we're beginning to smile.

Let's take a look at how dividends growing at 8 percent will affect our portfolio. Using the rule of 72, we can divide 72 by 8 (percent) and calculate the number of years it will take the dividends to double. 72/8 will give us 9 years. If we begin with a 3.5 percent dividend, we will double to 7 percent in 9 years. Our time frame is 10 years, so we have some time to spare, and as Table 22.5 shows (top to bottom), we should see a dividend return of 7.6 percent in the 10th year. Remember what Buffett says: "It is better to be approximately correct than precisely wrong."

Table 22.5 Tupperware TUP

Year	Projected Dividends
1	3.8%
2	4.1%
3	4.4%
4	4.8%
5	5.1%
6	5.6%
7	6.0%
8	6.5%
9	7.0%
10	7.6%

Please understand up to this point, we are merely considering the growth of the dividends of the individual companies over a 10-year period. However, we must also consider the reinvestment of those dividends into stocks that are paying dividends. We will reinvest those dividends either into the same companies or into other companies that fit our criteria.

If we begin by structuring a portfolio that is generating, say 3 percent per year in dividends, then the reinvestment of those dividends will increase the overall dividend rate by about 35 percent over 10 years. Think compounding! In other words, if dividends increase by 8 percent per year, the dividends will double in 9 years. This is the rule of 72. If we begin the first year with 3 percent in dividends, we will be returning double or 6 percent in 9 years. If we reinvest those dividends in our dividend-paying stocks, we will be returning about 7.5 percent in 10 years on original capital invested. If we begin at a rate of 3.5 percent, and we reinvest the dividends for 10 years, we could see an 8 percent dividend rate of return on our original invested capital.

Remember, we want to form a portfolio of dividend-paying stocks that are growing their dividends in the high single digits. Let's pick a target dividend growth rate of about 8 percent.

We are not counting the growth or increase in price of the stocks over our 10-year period. This is what the next chapter is all about. Read on.

SUMMARY

We want a portfolio made up of stocks that are growing their dividends 7 percent to 8 percent per year. We want our dividend income to at least double over the next 10 years.

Chapter 23

A Great Dividend Income and Growth Strategy—Part III: Selecting Stocks That Are Growing in Price for Our Portfolio

T he last chapter told us how to find the dividend growth rate so that we may select stocks that fit our portfolio criteria of grow-ing their dividends approximately 8 percent per year.

This chapter will help us determine the future growth rate of a stock after dividends are accounted for. We need the growth rate of a stock in order to achieve our goal of selecting stocks that not only have an 8 percent dividend growth rate, but also have a 7 percent price growth rate as well.

We want to strive to select stocks that will double in value (price) over the next 10 years. Just a note here: Price does not always follow value in the short term; however, price does indeed follow value over the long term. Value is the worth or the profitable projects a company builds (or buys) over the years. Price, which can change every minute of every day, is in the minds of the beholders, but value is something very real and it is something that good companies build over the long term.

> We want the stocks in our portfolio to double in price over the next 10 years.

During the market crash of 1987, the market (Dow) fell 22 percent in one day. Actually, the price of stocks in the Dow on average fell 22 percent, but the *value* of those stocks did not fall except in the minds of those large money managers who felt they needed to stay liquid. Eventually, price caught back up to the intrinsic (basic) value of those companies. As a matter of fact, the market actually closed the year (1987) higher than it began. Those who sold at the bottom were very sad puppies indeed. The market is now 950 percent higher today than the end of the day of October 19, 1987.

> The rule of 72 is the doubling rule. If you want to know at what percentage growth rate a stock or portfolio will double in value, divide the number of years into 72.

Using the rule of 72, we want to find the growth rate needed in a portfolio of stocks in order to double in value within our 10-year time frame. Thus, 72/10 = 7.2 percent. This means we must select stocks that

> Do not confuse the *dividend* growth rate with the growth rate of the stock itself. We are looking for stocks that grow their dividends by 8 percent per year, but we also want those stocks to increase in value (price) at a rate of 7–8 percent per year.

are growing in value (and thus price) at 7.2 percent per year. If we can accomplish this, then we will see a doubling of our portfolio value in 10 years. We are not counting dividends in this chapter. We are just looking at the value (price) of our stock portfolio, and we are trying to select stocks that will double in value over the next 10 years.

The growth of a company is dependent on the value of the projects or investments that a company makes over time. The money for these projects comes from earnings reinvested back into the company or from the money a company borrows. We can measure the success of these investments by calculating a return on equity (ROE) in a Clean Surplus condition. If a company continues to generate a high ROE, then we know that the company is earning a high rate of return on its investments and projects.

We have learned in this book that a method of measuring earnings efficiency is using the Clean Surplus ROE.

We have also learned that the Clean Surplus ROE has a very good correlation with the future growth (price) of a company.

Let's look at an example. If the average stock in the S&P 500 Index has a Clean Surplus ROE of 14 percent and a growth stock we select has an ROE of 28 percent, we would expect to see our growth stock double the returns of the market as measured by the S&P 500 Index. Yes, it is that simple. Well almost.

Let's say that our growth stock pays out half of its earnings in the form of dividends. This means that if the stock has an ROE of 28 percent and pays half of the earnings out to shareholders in the form of dividends, then it is putting just half of the earnings back into the company in order to grow.

Putting it another way, the company is retaining half or 50 percent of its earnings in order to grow the company. If the ROE is 28 percent and the retention rate of its earnings (retained earnings) is 50 percent, then we are left with a projected 14 percent per year rate of future price growth.

We want to be able to measure the stock growth rate so we can compare one stock against another stock for portfolio selection.

> An ROE of 28 percent multiplied by a 50 percent retention rate = 14 percent potential growth rate of the stock (price) going into the future. Or, ROE times Retention Rate = Stock Growth Rate.
>
> I would like you all to remember that the Clean Surplus ROE is a bottom-line number. This ratio tells us just about all we need to know about a stock.

Philip Morris International

The first stock we looked at in the last chapter relative to dividend growth rate was Philip Morris International. Table 23.1 shows what we saw.

Table 23.1 Philip Morris International NYSE - PM 4.4%

Year	CS Owners' Equity	Net Income	Dividends Paid	Dividend Growth
2015	$13.06	$5.60	$4.24	8.7%
2014	$11.86	$5.10	$3.90	8.9%
2013	$10.18	$5.26	$3.58	10.5%
2012	$8.25	$5.17	$3.24	14.9%
2011	$6.22	$4.85	$2.82	15.6%
2010	$4.74	$3.92	$2.44	8.9%
2009	$3.74	$3.24	$2.24	124.0%
2008	$1.42	$3.32	$1.00	

Let's now look at some more statistics in Table 23.2

In Table 23.2 we see the ROE of 43 percent for 2015. We also see the retention rate of 24 percent for this same year. This means that out of the $5.60 of net income, the dividends are $4.24 and the retained earnings then must be $1.36. This $1.36 of retained earnings (earnings put back into the company) divided by the net income of $5.60 is the retention rate of 24 percent.

Table 23.2   Philip Morris International - PM 4.4%

Year	Net Income	Dividends Paid	Retained Earnings	Return on Equity	Retention Rate	Stock Growth
2015	$5.60	$4.24	$1.36	43%	24%	10%
2014	$5.10	$3.90	$1.20	43%	24%	10%
2013	$5.26	$3.58	$1.68	52%	32%	17%
2012	$5.17	$3.24	$1.93	63%	37%	23%
2011	$4.85	$2.82	$2.03	78%	42%	33%
2010	$3.92	$2.44	$1.48	83%	38%	31%
2009	$3.24	$2.24	$1.00	87%	31%	27%

Retained earnings ($1.36) divided by net income ($5.60) = retention rate (24 percent).

We know that if this company did not pay out any dividends, then the ROE is a very good indicator of future growth (price). In this case, we would expect a stock growth rate of almost 43 percent. Whew, right? However, we must take into consideration the dividends. The dividends for Philip Morris represent about 76 percent of the earnings. How did I calculate that? The percentage of dividends paid (76 percent) subtracted from 100 percent is the retention rate.

What isn't put back into the company is paid out in the form of dividends. The percentage of dividends plus the percentage of retained earnings must equal 100 percent.

But, we are concerned with the growth rate of the stock. For 2015, we merely take the Clean Surplus ROE (43 percent) and multiply it by the retention rate (24 percent), and this equals the last column for 2015 of 10 percent. Thus, we can expect this stock to grow in price about 10 percent per year.

For Philip Morris International we have a dividend of 4.2 percent, which is growing at a dividend growth rate of 8.7 percent and a projected stock growth (price) rate of 10.4 percent. I don't know about you, but this stock is going into our dividend income and growth portfolio.

The percentage of dividends paid (76 percent) subtracted from 100 percent is the retention rate. 100% − 76% = 24%; 24% of net income ($5.60) = $1.36.

Note: These numbers are rounded off.

AT&T

We saw earlier that AT&T had a nice high dividend of 5.3 percent. However, we also saw that the dividend growth rate was a mere 2.2 percent, which is certainly not good enough for our portfolio (see Table 23.3).

But maybe, just maybe, the stock growth rate (price) might be high enough to justify the low dividend growth rate. NOT! See Table 23.4.

Remember how this is done. We take the ROE, which is a good indication of the future total return of a stock and multiply it by the retention rate. The retention rate is how much money the company puts back into itself in order to grow.

The ROE (7 percent) times retention rate (33 percent), or 0.7 times 0.33, gives us the anticipated stock growth rate listed in Table 23.4 for 2015 of just 2 percent.

Let's analyze. The dividend is very good at 5.3 percent. The dividend growth of 2.2 percent does not meet our criteria of a 7–8 percent growth rate. The stock growth of 2 percent does not meet our criteria of

Table 23.3   AT&T, Inc. NYSE - T Div. 5.3%

Year	CS Owners' Equity	Net Income	Dividends Paid	Dividend Growth
2015	$42.28	$2.80	$1.88	2.2%
2014	$41.52	$2.60	$1.84	2.2%
2013	$40.82	$2.50	$1.80	2.3%
2012	$40.25	$2.33	$1.76	2.3%
2011	$39.77	$2.20	$1.72	2.4%
2010	$39.16	$2.29	$1.68	2.4%
2009	$38.68	$2.12	$1.64	2.5%
2008	$38.12	$2.16	$1.60	12.7%
2007	$36.78	$2.76	$1.42	

Table 23.4   AT&T, Inc. NYSE - T

Year	Net Income	Dividends Paid	Retained Earnings	Return on Equity	Retention Rate	Stock Growth
2015	$2.80	$1.88	$0.92	7%	33%	2%
2014	$2.60	$1.84	$0.76	6%	29%	2%
2013	$2.50	$1.80	$0.70	6%	28%	2%
2012	$2.33	$1.76	$0.57	6%	24%	1%
2011	$2.20	$1.72	$0.48	6%	22%	1%
2010	$2.29	$1.68	$0.56	6%	26%	1%
2009	$2.12	$1.64	$1.34	8%	49%	4%

a 7 percent stock growth rate. Bottom line with AT&T: This company will just not get us to where we want to be in 10 years.

A Pretty Good Portfolio Stock

I was looking through stocks for a seminar I was presenting to about 100 CPAs. Clean Surplus is approved by various accounting agencies as certification for continuing education credits. When I am asked to present, I try and find new examples and in doing so for this presentation, I came across Tupperware. Yes, you all remember Tupperware. We went over this stock just in part so let's continue on with it. First, let's recheck the dividend and dividend growth shown in Table 23.5.

We see the dividend is 3.3 percent, which is pretty close to our desired overall portfolio requirement of 3.5 percent. Also from Table 23.5

Table 23.5   Tupperware - TUP 3.3%

Year	Dividends Paid	Dividend Growth
2015	$3.00	10%
2014	$2.72	10%
2013	$2.48	72%
2012	$1.44	20%
2011	$1.20	20%
2010	$1.00	10%
2009	$0.91	3%

we see the dividend growth rate of 10 percent, which is above our requirement of dividend growth.

From Table 23.6 we are able to calculate the stock growth rate for 2015. Using the 2015 row, we see the net income to be $6.10. From that amount, Tupperware is retaining or putting back into the company 51 percent in order to continue to grow.

In order to determine the potential stock growth rate, we take the ROE (29 percent) and multiply it by the retention rate (51 percent), or 0.29 times 0.51, which gives us an expected stock growth rate (last column for 2015) of 0.15 or 15 percent, which is pretty darn good.

Table 23.6   Tupperware Brands NYSE - TUP Div. 3.3%

Year	Net Income	Dividends Paid	Retained Earnings	Return on Equity	Retention Rate	Stock Growth
2015	$6.10	$3.00	$3.10	29%	51%	15%
2014	$5.00	$2.72	$2.28	27%	46%	12%
2013	$5.17	$2.48	$2.69	32%	52%	17%
2012	$3.42	$1.44	$1.98	24%	58%	14%
2011	$3.55	$1.20	$2.35	30%	66%	20%
2010	$3.53	$1.00	$2.53	38%	72%	27%
2009	$2.75	$0.91	$1.84	37%	67%	25%

Let's analyze. The dividend is good at 3.3 percent. The dividend growth of 10 percent is above our criteria of 7–8 percent. The stock growth of 15 percent is above our criteria of 7 percent. Bottom line: If Tupperware can continue to earn enough money in order to fund both the dividend growth and the company growth, this company is a wonderful candidate for our dividend and growth portfolio.

One thing to notice is the Clean Surplus ROE (see Table 23.7).

Since 2011, the ROE has remained around 30 percent. Always remember that the ROE means the company is earning a 29 percent (for 2015) return on the money it reinvested not only in the distant past, but also on the money it reinvested back into the company last year. The more consistent the Clean Surplus ROE, the better we can be assured that Tupperware will continue to earn a good return for shareholders going into the future. This is a very good thing.

Table 23.7 Tupperware - ROE

Year	ROE
2015	29%
2014	27%
2013	32%
2012	24%
2011	30%
2010	38%
2009	37%

We've learned to look for the growth in the dividend and the growth in the stock in order to meet our 10-year objectives. However, there is something else we like to add to our portfolio in order to make it a stellar performing portfolio that will grow and create income far and above all the other portfolios out there in Investment Land without taking on undue risk. You are about to enter the world of "enhanced income." If we haven't knocked your socks off yet, read on.

SUMMARY

When selecting a stock for our Dividend Income and Growth portfolio, we want to look at the dividend growth rate as well as the anticipated stock growth rate. The reason is we want not only to see a doubling of dividends paid out to us in 10 years, but we also want to see the value of the stocks in our portfolio double in 10 years. This is a wonderful and achievable goal.

Chapter 24

Enhanced Income

W e've constructed some very nice portfolios so far. A growth portfolio can be constructed with the use of our computer program in very little time. You merely find the stocks that have high and consistent Clean Surplus ROEs. Some stocks have rising ROEs, which is even better.

We then went on to develop a great dividend income and growth portfolio: a little more work, but wow, what a great portfolio and easy to maintain.

But what if we can take those two fantastic portfolios and add another 2, 3, or 4 percent per year to either portfolio?

What if we take our two great portfolios and are able to add another 3–4 percent per year to each of them? "Wow" is the word you are looking for.

We can put some of this added income into the purchase of insurance or just reinvest that extra income each year or a little of both. More work, yes, but just think about the reward at the end of the rainbow.

This chapter will give us a basic understanding of the concept of enhanced income. This chapter is not intended to teach you the various methods of adding income, as that would take books and not chapters. It also takes time and experience. We can always head you in the direction of people who do this for a living, but for now, let's just talk about the concept of enhanced income.

I first heard the term "enhanced income" from a dear friend, formerly of Smith Barney. It simply means ways to increase the income of a portfolio through such methods as covered option writing as well as option spread strategies. If you can take the time to master some of these extra-income techniques, you can position yourself way ahead of all other growth or dividend income and growth portfolios throughout the land. We can also use this added income to help pay for portfolio insurance, which we'll talk about in the next chapter, but for now, let's just talk about adding income to our dividend income and growth portfolio.

Can we generate another 4 percent per year to the portfolio through enhanced income?

I've been using enhanced income methods for over 30 years. As you read this chapter on enhanced income, you will see there are several methods used to generate income.

If we are able to generate and then reinvest another 4 percent per year in our portfolio, we can increase the value of the portfolio by another 48 percent over a 10-year time frame. I merely used my Excel spreadsheet and projected what a certain amount of money would be worth in 10 years at a growth rate of 4 percent. Of course, all financial calculators are equipped to calculate the time value of money going into the future. But the important thing is that generating another 48 percent *on top* of the doubling of the value of the portfolio (after 10 years) due to the stocks themselves growing at 7–8 percent per year becomes a very sizeable portfolio increase of approximately 150 percent.

Wait a minute, you say? Let's add everything up as this is beginning to sound like a wonderful use of compounding, especially in our Dividend Income and Growth portfolio:

1. We are buying stocks that are growing at about 7 percent per year. This alone can double the value of a portfolio in 10 years.
2. We are buying stocks that are increasing their dividends 7 percent to 8 percent per year, which means our dividend stream will more than double in 10 years through the use of reinvestment (compounding).
3. Finally, we may be able to add another 4 percent per year to the portfolio through enhanced income, which in and of itself can add almost 50 percent of value to the portfolio over a 10-year period.

In summary so far, if we invest $100,000 and if we meet all our objectives, we could have a portfolio worth two and a half times ($250,000) the starting value ($100,000) in 10 years, which will be generating anywhere from 8 percent to 9 percent in dividends on the original amount. This is assuming we begin the portfolio with stocks presently generating 3.5 percent in dividends today.

With our 4 percent per year of enhanced income, the yearly income generated in 10 years will be the 8 percent to 9 percent in dividends plus another 4 percent of enhanced income for total income of 12 percent to 13 percent per year.

Just a note here: Does this sound like some of the annuities that are out there in Investment Land? There is one annuity at the time this book is written that will pay you 8 percent per year for life after a 10-year holding period. Now you are beginning to understand how they do it. The only problem with the annuity I'm familiar with is that you don't have control of your money and your original investment will never grow. This means YOU never see the growth. Gee, I wonder who gets the appreciation in the portfolio? Not you.

However, with the investment we are speaking about, you have control of your money. Why? Because it is your money. With our strategy, your income could exceed 12 percent per year after 10 years, and your portfolio could more than double. That's the difference between you investing or having an annuity company invest for you.

Covered Option Writing

This is not a chapter designed to teach you how to master the skill of covered option writing. Rather, it is designed to acquaint you with one of the strategies I like to use to gain some extra income within my own personal portfolio. Or to say it another way, I am enhancing the return of my portfolio. Thus the term "enhanced income."

This chapter is to merely alert you to the fact that different people use different enhanced income methods. To me, the best strategy is to buy and hold the stocks in my portfolio.

I once taught some folks the art and science of option writing. They wanted to earn an extra 4 percent per year on a growth portfolio. Here's what they worked out.

If the stocks in their portfolios returned 9 percent per year on average, the portfolio would double in value every eight years. With an extra 4 percent (13 percent total portfolio return), the portfolio would double in just five-and-a-half years (not shown). Let's see what that extra 4 percent per year does to an average growth stock portfolio (see Table 24.1).

Look at the long-term outcome if you can gain just another 4 percent per year in your portfolio. You could retire in 24 years with almost $800,000 at a return of 9 percent per year, or you can retire in the same amount of time (24 years) with more than double the $800,000 if you can earn a total 13 percent per year return. Let's see, $800,000 or $1,900,000?

What Does This Have to Do with Options?

There are many, many different strategies relative to options. You can use them for leverage, or you can take the opposite position and use them for income while at the same time making your portfolio a bit more conservative.

Table 24.1   Compounding an Extra 4 Percent per Year

	At 9%	At 13%
	$100,000	$100,000
8 years	$200,000	$266,000
16 years	$400,000	$707,000
24 years	$800,000	$1,900,000

Many people believe option strategies are a form of gambling, and they liken options to a gambling casino. But if you think about it, the casino, or house, makes money from the thousands of gamblers who, on average, lose money. Gambling is based on probability. Somebody loses and somebody wins. The game of chance in a casino is tilted toward the casino winning just a few more times than the gambler. The question is would you rather be the gambler or the house? The gambler could make a killing, but most times he or she will lose all their money. The house makes a few dollars at a time. Does the casino actually make money? The Las Vegas and Macau casinos are still very much in business. Therefore, they must be making money more times than not in the short term, and in the long term, definitely.

How does this apply to stocks? Covered option writing (selling call options) guarantees you will make income from selling an option (conservative position) to the option buyer (gambler). "Covered" means you own the underlying stock.

We can look at the option buyer as the gambler and you, the seller, as the house. You are giving the gambler, user of leverage, the opportunity to make a lot of money relative to the amount of money he or she has invested.

A call option gives the buyer (gambler) of that option the right to purchase a stock (from you) at a certain predetermined, agreed-upon price (strike price) within a certain amount of time.

Think of a call option as a contract that has three parts: the time involved, the agreed-upon price they can buy the stock from you (strike price), and the cost of the option which goes to you the seller.

Here's an example. If it is now June with Home Depot at $30 per share and you sell a Home Depot July 30 call option for $1, you, the seller, now have a dollar in your pocket. The buyer of the option (gambler) just paid you $1 per share for the right to buy your stock from you at $30 per share between now and the third Friday in July. (The third Friday of the month is option expiration day.) Just a note here: There are now weekly options, which makes this strategy even more exciting for you, the option seller.

What? Give Up My Stock? Shame on You!

Something is wrong here. You just limited the upside potential on your stock. Yes, you did receive $1 per share, which you get to keep no matter what happens, but if Home Depot goes to $35 within the month, you are obligated to sell your stock at $30 per share. This doesn't sound like much fun, does it? Well, the following strategy allows you to keep your stock, but first, a few quick basics.

A Few Basics

An option contract is based upon 100 shares of stock. Everyone uses terminology relative to a per share basis, but all prices are based on a "round lot" of 100 shares. Earlier I mentioned an option price of $1 per share. This means that each option on each share is worth $1. Since we must deal in round lots of 100 shares, we are really speaking about 100 shares of Home Depot. The option contract of $1 per share for 100 shares is $100. Simply multiply everything by 100.

But I Want to Keep My Stock

Yes, when I find some good stocks, I want to keep them and not have them called away from me. If I sell my stocks before a year is up, I then pay Uncle Sam extra money, and I really don't want to generate discretionary income for him. I want to pay him just enough for him to get by. So let's not make our "uncle" more of a partner in our endeavors than is necessary.

A Bit of Technical Analysis

One thing to remember is that you have all year to generate 4 percent through the use of option writing. This is where a little technical analysis comes in handy. Just so you are aware, technical analysis is a very handy tool. However, it does not work all the time. It does work some of the time, which is the time we are concerned with. There are many formations, one if which is a double top. Another is a reversal in trend, which also may include a double top. Here are my simple rules:

1. Make sure the stock upon which you are selling a covered call on is not paying a dividend within the next month.
2. Look for stocks that are changing trends or forming a double top.

3. Look if the market itself (Dow or the S&P 500 index) is either in or beginning a "down" trend.

4. 4) Sell a covered call on half your stock position (in case you are wrong) no more than a month out. I personally like to sell just a one- or two-week call.

Keeping your rules to a minimum and not getting greedy will allow you to sell covered calls with a small chance of having your stock called away from you. If you keep the time short (two weeks rather than two months) for your option writes, you will have a greater control over your stock because if you are wrong, you won't be so wrong that your stock can "get away" from you if it goes higher.

There are many other option strategies such as butterflies and iron butterflies, condors and iron condors, bull and bear spreads, calendar spreads, and so on.

SUMMARY

We just wanted to whet your appetite a bit and let you know that people out there make a very nice living using options in order to generate extra income for their portfolios. We also want to let you know there are money managers out there who do a very nice job in this area. For those of you who insist on managing your own portfolios, you might think twice about letting an expert handle this part of your portfolio. The experts we recommend for option writing also know how to hedge your portfolio, which is why you should read the next chapter sooner rather than later.

Chapter 25

Portfolio Insurance

I nsurance, or hedging, is something we hear about an awful lot, but
what does it mean relative to our world of investing? A good place
to begin is using the following definition: Hedging is making an
investment in order to reduce the risk of an adverse (very bad) price
move in our portfolio.

When you think of a portfolio or stock hedge, think of your car
insurance. Let's say you buy a $20,000 car and of course, before you drive
that car out of the dealer's parking lot, you really want to have insurance
on that vehicle. If you took out a loan in order to purchase that car, the
folks lending you the money will insist you have insurance in order to
protect their loan to you.

We just touched on one very important point. We want to protect
the money we spent on that car whether it is our own money or somebody else's money. If we borrowed the money as most of us do when
purchasing a large ticket item, we want to protect ourselves against a
devastating event. After all, if a tree falls on our car while it is sitting in

our driveway, we will no longer have a car, and we will still owe $20,000
to the nice folks who loaned us that money. By the way, those nice folks
won't be so nice when they try and collect money from you, and you
don't have it to give to them.

Back to insurance: If we had insurance on our car and the car becomes worthless because of a devastating event, the insurance company
will pay back those nice folks who loaned us the $20,000. Then every-
one can go on their merry way with only the inconvenience of searching for another car to replace the one that was destroyed.

A fairly new term has come about in the world of investing, and it
is called "tactical investing." Tactical investing is nothing new. It merely
means that when a portfolio manager feels that the market will decline, he
or she will begin to rotate your portfolio into defensive types of stocks or
they may even begin to sell the holdings in your portfolio. Another tactic
they may use is to purchase a security that will gain in value as the market
goes down. Tactical asset managers will use one or all of these methods as
well as any other method they may see fit in order to protect a portfolio.

What is the problem with selling securities in anticipation of a market decline? First of all, selling securities because of a perceived decline
in the market causes a taxable event in most portfolios. Should the market instead go up and the portfolio manager has sold some or all of the
securities in a portfolio, the manager could exhibit a sickening feeling
in the bottom of his stomach as he watches his portfolio *not* participate
in the market rally.

> Remember, the second worst fear of a money manager is to be
> out of the market when the market goes up.

What in the world can be worse than the fear of being out of the
market while the market continues to go up, you ask? I'll tell you what.

There are securities available that increase in value when the market
declines. This can be in the form of selling a futures contract on the S&P
500 Index or any other index. Another security that will increase in
value as the market declines is an instrument with the symbol SDS. The
SDS is the Proshares Ultrashort S&P 500, which seeks daily investment

results that corresponds to *two times* the inverse of the daily performance of the S&P 500 index. In other words, this security will go up twice as fast on a percentage basis as the market goes down. The problem with the SDS is that it will go down twice as fast as the market should the market go up rather than go down.

We have just set the stage to understand what the single worst fear in portfolio management may be. The absolute worst fear in the entire world of investing is to be wrong about the market direction and at the same time be in some type of security that is actually losing money while the market is going up. Yes, losing money when the market is going up is much worse than not making money while the market is going up.

> The very worst fear of a money manager (or you) is to be in a hedging instrument that is going down in value while the market is going up.

What Does Buffett Do?

We all know what Buffett does. He buys when the market is at its worst. And somehow, he always seems to have money available when the market goes down. At what seems to be the worst time in the market, he is brave enough to enter the market when it seems the world is falling apart.

So What Can We Do?

Yes, I know, none of us ever seem to have money available when the market is falling apart. And since we are human, we are very scared when the market falls day after day because we are thinking defensively during severe market declines rather than thinking offensively. In other words, we are screaming to get out when we should be thinking of looking for the opportunity to buy more of our favorite stocks.

Ok, So What Can We Do to Take the Guessing out of Investing?

I like to buy insurance on my portfolio. If I have the same type of insurance on the portfolio as I do on my car, I will have protection on my portfolio *at all times*. If the market and my portfolio experience a serious decline, then my insurance will increase in value as my portfolio decreases in value. When I want to cash in my insurance policy, my portfolio insurance will pay me in cash. Did you hear what I just said? *My portfolio insurance will pay me in cash.* Yes, I see that glimmer in your eyes. You need cash at market bottoms, and one certain type of portfolio insurance will pay you in cash when you need it most, which is, of course, after a serious market decline.

The Amazing Thing about Portfolio Insurance

The following analogy is guaranteed to blow your mind. We know in retrospect that every market decline is eventually followed by a market rebound. In other words, your portfolio, assuming you have good stocks, will eventually come back and even surpass the market value prior to the decline. And we all know that, eventually, your portfolio will become worth even more.

In direct contrast to your stock portfolio is your home insurance. If your home burns down, it will become a house again only if you take the money from your insurance and use it to rebuild your home.

But, with portfolio insurance, you can cash in your portfolio insurance near or at the market bottom and get cash. After the panic selling is over and confidence is once again restored relative to the economy, both the market and your portfolio will once again be worth what it was before the crash. And the amazing thing is you will still have the cash from your portfolio insurance. *Are you getting this?*

If you look at this scenario and act the way a real professional would act, you can cash in your portfolio insurance somewhere near the bottom and use that cash to buy more of your favorite stocks. You will then have up to twice as many of your favorite stocks. Then, when the market rebounds to pre-crash levels, your portfolio will be worth *twice as much* as it was before.

This is how you build wealth! Oops, I didn't mean to yell this out across the universe, but just think about doubling your portfolio value after the market merely regains its pre-crash value.

Market Crash Mentality

Everybody hates a market crash. Some of you will speak about short sellers or traders who make money while the market is going down. Allow me to speak about these folks and market crashes. During severe market declines, there are usually three distinct down legs. If there are three distinct declines, there are three distinct market rebounds. These rebound rallies are vicious, and those short sellers panic after seeing their profits from the declining market evaporate within a few days or a few hours. Unless a short seller understands that there will be rallies followed by deeper declines and know enough to hold on to their short positions, they will not make nearly as much money as most people think. I know this is surprising to you, but trust me on this because you are hearing this from the horse's mouth.

Back to the Crash Mentality

If you have portfolio insurance *and* the market is crashing, guess what? You really don't care what happens. If you are hedged properly, your portfolio value is not declining. Yes, your stocks are losing value, but the increase in value of your portfolio insurance is increasing. If this is so, then you can go to the beach and not even care what the market is doing.

As the market goes through its gyrations, you will be able to look at the market with a totally different mentality. You will be able to keep your head when all those around you are losing theirs. Yes, you've heard this phrase before. It's from Rudyard Kipling's poem about a young boy becoming a man.

Which Scenario Do You Prefer?

Do you prefer total panic or cool, calm, and collected? I'm not even going to insult your intelligence by having you answer this question because I already know the answer. Cool, calm, and collected allows you to make good, practical choices. Panicking does not. And as Forrest Gump says, "That's all I have to say about tha-at."

> You insure your life, you insure your house, you insure your possessions, and you insure your health, so why don't you insure your stock portfolio?

Before I go further, I want to remind you that you insure your life, you insure your house, you insure your possessions, and you insure your health. You insure all those things that are very difficult or impossible to replace. My question is, Why don't you insure your stock portfolio?
You very probably insure your other investments such as your investment in real estate or collectible paintings, stamps, and coins. You certainly insure those investment apartments you bought in order to garner that monthly rental income.

If you invested in a business, you insure your business assets and you will very probably insure any interruption in your business for any reason (business interruption insurance). However, you can have millions of dollars in the stock market, and you don't insure your portfolio in the event of a serious market decline.

How Do We Insure Our Portfolios?

My favorite method of insurance is to purchase index put options in an amount approximately equal to the value of my portfolio.

First of all, what is a "put option"? A put option is just like your car insurance. You can buy car insurance for, say, $1,000 per year on your $20,000 car, and you will receive (almost) $20,000 if disaster strikes your car within the time frame of the insurance policy.

Just like car insurance, you can buy insurance on individual stocks or you can buy insurance on various marked indices such as the S&P 500 Index.

> My favorite method of insurance is to purchase index put options in an amount approximately equal to the value of my portfolio.

However, it is very difficult and time consuming trying to buy insurance on each stock in a 20- or 30-stock portfolio. An easier and more cost-efficient method of insuring a portfolio is to insure "the market." One way to insure "the market" is to purchase put options on either the S&P 100 index or the S&P 500 index. These options are called index put options. There are many other index options, but for now let's concentrate on the S&P 100 and S&P 500.

Cash, Cash, Cash

The one fantastic thing about our index options (both calls and puts) is that they settle in cash. At this point we are just discussing put options, which are the same as our insurance policy on our car or house.

Settling in cash means that when the options expire, or the insurance contract period is over and there was no significant market decline (no car accident), the insurance contract just expires worthless. However, if there was a severe market decline (big car accident), the index put option will pay you a certain amount of CASH!

But How Much Cash?

Just like your car, it depends on the damage to the market. The cash payout will depend on the amount of market damage, minus the deductible.

Let's take the car. If we have a $2,000 deductible on a $20,000 car and the tree falling on our car caused $10,000 worth of damage, the insurance company will pay us the amount of the damage ($10,000) minus the deductible of $2,000 or a total payout in cash of $8,000.

Why is it so important to have cash when the market declines? It is important to have cash at or near market bottoms so you can purchase more of your favorite stocks at bargain prices. This is exactly how a very few of the famous people of Wall Street became rich. Of course, there are multitudes of people who never had insurance (or forgot to sell) during market declines and went bankrupt.

If we insure our portfolio with a 10 percent deductible and the market drops 25 percent, then our insurance will pay us the 25 percent market decline minus the 10 percent deductible or a total cash payout of

15 percent. Of course, if the market drops to zero, then the insurance or put option will pay us 90 percent of the portfolio value.

Now we know that the market will probably never, ever drop to zero, but when the market gets into free fall, it sure seems as though it is going to drop to zero. It is in times like these that we are very happy we have portfolio insurance.

> When the market seems as though it is going down forever, we are very happy we have portfolio insurance.

A problem with insuring the market is your portfolio may not correlate 100 percent with the market. One hundred percent correlation means your portfolio will move exactly as the market moves. Some portfolios are more risky than the S&P 100 or S&P 500 index. Thus, when the market goes into free fall, the portfolio may decline more than the general market, but your insurance is covering the market and not the individual stocks in the portfolio.

Just a point here: Buffett made all his big money in the large companies. Knowing he is a multibillionaire, why do you want to invest in those small companies you hear about at the water fountain? It may be a good idea to wait until those small companies become medium-size or larger, and you can still make money like Buffett. In fact, you can make more money than Buffett if you buy good stocks and insure your portfolio.

Back to correlation with the market: If your portfolio is made up mostly of S&P 500 stocks or Dow stocks, then you will probably correlate fairly well with the market when the market is in decline mode. In other words, invest a bit like Buffett.

Back to our portfolio insurance: Think of your car insurance again. We usually don't insure our cars for full value because it just plain costs too much. With a $20,000 car we usually find that a $1,000 or $2,000 deductible policy is "almost" affordable. I know, I know, any type of insurance is expensive, but insurance is very necessary.

How about a 10 percent deductible on the portfolio just like most car insurance policies? You see, if we try and insure a portfolio at full value, it could cost us about 10 percent to 12 percent per year. However, we all know that on average, the market returns somewhere from 10 percent to 12 percent per year. That means in order to fully insure or hedge a portfolio, the cost of insurance will almost be the exact amount of profit the market will give us in any "average" year. In other words, we will never make money in the market if we fully insure.

However, if we insure our portfolios with put options at about 10 percent below market value (think 10 percent deductible on your car insurance) or looking at it another way, if we are happy with insuring approximately 90 percent of our portfolio, our cost will drop to anywhere from 2 percent to 4 percent per year depending on market conditions.

What Do We Mean by Market Conditions?

Think of trying to get hurricane insurance in New Orleans just when a hurricane has formed in the Gulf of Mexico and is heading straight for the Louisiana coast. Now think of purchasing portfolio insurance when world events cause a scare around the world and everyone is running for cover at the same time. A properly insured portfolio is constantly adjusting the insurance mainly because the value of the portfolio is constantly changing. Thus, there will be times when portfolio insurance is not so expensive, and then there will be times when the insurance is very expensive.

SUMMARY

The big question is how do we pay for portfolio insurance? You already know the answer because hopefully you already read the chapter on enhanced income. You certainly don't want to take the cost of portfolio insurance out of portfolio appreciation. You want to pay for your insurance from the little extra income you generate within your portfolio. And folks, you can take that bit of information all the way to the bank.

Chapter 26

What Have You Learned? A Summary

I'm sure by now you are well aware there is a lot of information in this book. I have shared with you my many years of academic research. I'm also sharing with you over 33 years of actual stock market experience. You learned how Warren Buffett uses Clean Surplus Accounting to project a stock's price 10 years into the future. You then learned how he discounts that future, target price back to the present, which in turn determines his all-important purchase price.

Using a combination of Buffett's method and my research work, you are now aware that you need to fill your portfolios with stocks that have high and consistent returns on equity (ROEs), with that ROE configured by Clean Surplus Accounting.

We saw in the published doctoral dissertation research that portfolios consisting of stocks with high ROEs outperformed portfolios that consisted of lower ROEs.

A random selection of 122 stocks that were asked about by our radio listeners showed the same findings that the doctoral dissertation research showed. Portfolios consisting of stocks with higher ROEs outperformed portfolios made up of stocks with lower ROEs.

Our model portfolio over the past 12 years has outperformed the S&P 500 index by over a two-to-one margin and also outperformed Buffett's Berkshire Hathaway portfolio by almost the same amount.

> Portfolios consisting of stocks with higher ROEs outperformed portfolios made up of stocks with lower ROEs.

Let's review what you have learned but first please remember that in order to compare one company to another, we must first use accounting numbers that are calculated the exact same way between all companies. This is what Clean Surplus allows us to do. Only when Clean Surplus is used can we construct a truly comparable operating efficiency ratio and here is why:

1. The ROE ratio is a ratio used to measure the operating efficiency of a company.
2. It is the most widely accepted ratio used for comparing the operating efficiency of one company relative to the operating efficiency of another company.
3. However, most of the investing, financial, and accounting professionals calculate the ratio in a manner not conducive to the comparison of operating efficiencies *between* different companies. In other words, they use the traditional accounting ROE, which does not lend itself to predictability. It is for this reason that the accounting profession developed Clean Surplus Accounting.
4. Most finance professionals use earnings from the income statement for the return portion of ROE and book value from the balance sheet for the equity portion of the ROE ratio.
5. However, the earnings number from the income statement contains non-recurring items, which are unique only to an individual company. These non-recurring items do not lend themselves to predictability because they do not occur in a predictable fashion.

6. The earnings number is the tie-in between the income statement and the balance sheet. The balance sheet contains the book value (owners' equity).

7. If the earnings number becomes distorted because of non-recurring items, then the earnings number will in turn distort the book value (owners' equity) on the balance sheet.

8. If parts of a ratio (earnings and book value) contain individual company items that are unique to one company and not common to all companies, then that ratio cannot be used for comparison of one company to another company.

9. Most of the investing world is using the wrong (traditional accounting) ROE, which is not a comparable nor predictable ratio (Figure 26.1). This is exactly why the accounting profession developed Clean Surplus. Thus, the investing world cannot truly compare companies relative to their operating efficiency if they are using a non-comparable ratio. This may be why most of the investing world cannot consistently outperform the market averages.

10. Clean Surplus Accounting is designed to leave out items which do not lend themselves to predictability.

11. Clean Surplus Accounting uses net income (earnings before non-recurring items) rather than earnings for the return portion of ROE (Figure 26.2). Net income is calculated in the same manner from company to company and does not contain items unique to one individual company and not another. Thus, it is a purer, more comparable number and certainly lends itself to predictability.

INCOME STATEMENT	BALANCE SHEET

Revenues
  Minus Expenses
	Assets
	  Minus Liabilities

= Net Income Minus Non-recurring items (Such as Extraordinary Losses and Future Liabilities)	= Book Value (Owners' Equity) (Common Stock + All Retained Earnings)
= Earnings	
Earnings – Dividends = Retained Earnings	

Figure 26.1   Traditional Accounting

INCOME STATEMENT	BALANCE SHEET
Revenues 　Minus Expenses	**Assets** 　Minus Liabilities
= Net Income 　　Minus Non-recurring Items (Such as Extraordinary Losses and Future Liabilities) **= Earnings**	**= Book Value (Owners' Equity)** (Common Stock + All Retained Earnings)

Figure 26.2　Clean Surplus Accounting

12. Clean Surplus Accounting calculates book value (owners' equity) using the true definition of owners' equity, which is the amount of money investors have put into the company through issuing common stock and adding all Clean Surplus retained earnings (profits), which is net income minus dividends.

13. Clean Surplus ROE thus configures both the return (net income) and equity (owners' equity) in the ROE ratio the exact same way for all companies.

14. If Clean Surplus ROE is configured in the exact same way for all companies, and it is, then Clean Surplus ROE and only Clean Surplus ROE may be used as a truly comparable efficiency ratio among all companies.

15. Published academic research work (*Clean Surplus Accounting: Value Relevance of Book Value and Earnings*, Dr. Joseph Belmonte, 2002) indicates there is a high correlation (association, connection, relationship) between the Clean Surplus ROE of a portfolio and the total future returns of that portfolio.

16. The published research contained in this book further shows that every portfolio that had a higher than average ROE outperformed the S&P 500 Index during the research test period.

Dividend Income and Growth Strategy

The research shows that the Clean Surplus ROE is a good indicator of the total return of a stock over the following four-year time period. If a stock has a Clean Surplus ROE of 20 percent and reinvests all that it

Table 26.1 Remember the Bank Account: This
Is Clean Surplus Accounting

Year	Equity	Interest	ROE
5	$146.00	$14.60	10.0%
4	$133.00	$13.30	10.0%
3	$121.00	$12.10	10.0%
2	**$110.00**	**$11.00**	10.0%
1	**$100.00**	**$10.00**	10.0%

earns back into the company for growth, we can make a pretty good
prediction that the stock will appreciate on average about 20 percent a
year over time. This is just like your bank account (Table 26.1). If your
bank is returning you 10 percent per year and you leave all your earnings (interest) in the bank, your account will grow 10 percent per year.

Back to our 20 percent ROE stock: If the company takes half of the
earnings and pays it out to shareholders in the form of dividends, then
the stock cannot grow at 20 percent. If the company pays half of the
earnings out to shareholders, then the maximum the stock can grow is
10 percent per year.

The key to our dividend income and growth strategy is being able
to measure the dividend growth rate and also to be able to predict the
approximate stock growth rate going into the future.

If this is so, then we can fill our dividend income and growth portfolio with stocks that are growing their dividends by 7–8 percent each
year as well as being able to fairly well predict if the stock growth rate is
also 8 percent or better.

> The Clean Surplus ROE can help us predict which stocks will grow
> both their earnings as well as their value (price) going into the future.

Portfolio Insurance and Enhanced Income

We learned that we are able to buy insurance policies on our portfolio
through the use of index put options. Think car insurance. Because car
insurance is so costly, we buy car insurance with a deductible. In other

words, we assume some of the risk of the first dollars of damage and let the insurance company assume the remaining, major portion of the risk.

Portfolio insurance is much the same. We try and insure about 90 percent of our portfolios because insuring 100 percent of the portfolio is much too costly.

Insuring 85 to 90 percent of a portfolio is still costly; however, we help to offset the cost of insurance through the use of certain enhanced income strategies. The most common form of enhanced income is the sale of covered options on some of our stocks.

We briefly mentioned that professionals like to use some form of technical analysis in order to sell covered calls so that their stocks will not be taken from the portfolio.

Putting the Odds of Success on My Side

Most of the readers of this book are very much like me. I want to put the odds of success on my side. Remember the definition of luck? When opportunity meets preparation. I feel you now have been sufficiently prepared to effectively take advantage of the opportunity that greets you through the understanding of this book. You are now one step ahead of most market analysts.

It wouldn't be mere luck if your portfolio continually outperforms the market averages in the future, because by reading this book, you are putting the odds of success on your side. The academic world will call you "lucky," but you know better. You are now prepared to garner the rewards of doing your homework. And we supply you the tools of outperformance through our computer program, the weekly video newsletter, and a host of educational video tutorials found on our website.

The next chapter will aid you in continuing your education. Through our website and a little help from your new friends at Buffett and Beyond Research, your portfolio will probably outperform almost everyone else over time. And since I know this to be true, I'm sure I'll soon see you at the beach. Move over, Jimmy and Warren B.

SUMMARY

It is our goal, through the understanding of our newly learned investment strategy, to invest successfully like Warren Buffett and then live just as we imagine the life enjoyed by Jimmy Buffett. Welcome to the beach.

Chapter 27

We Won't Leave You Out There Alone

www.wiley.com/go/buffettandbeyond

The great thing about this book is it doesn't leave you off at the bus stop in the middle of nowhere. Most of you don't want to worry about trying to obtain the accounting information needed to fill in the spreadsheets year after year. I don't blame you. We have everything you need for both your growth portfolio and your dividend income and growth portfolio. Everything can be accessed from our website, www.wiley.com/go/buffettandbeyond.

Once you purchase a copy of this book, just go to our website and fill in the form under the link "Contact Us" and tell us you purchased the book. We will give you an access code to the computer program and begin your subscription to the weekly video newsletter as well as a list of all the stocks presently in our portfolios. You will then be on your way.

Free with the purchase of this book: Four weeks of unlimited use of our computer program along with a 4-week trial of our weekly video newsletter. In addition you will also receive a list of all the stocks in our growth portfolio and also the stocks in our dividend income and growth portfolio.

The Weekly Video

Our weekly video contains three sections. The first is an update on the market using charts and technical analysis. We discuss where the market is at the present time and what are the probabilities of where we may be going over the following week.

The second section is an analysis of several growth and/or income stocks using the Clean Surplus analysis contained in this book. This section uses the computer program so you may learn how to effectively use the program to its fullest capacity on your own for stocks or stocks that you hear about.

The third section shows the put option positions used to hedge our portfolios as well as how we use covered option writing in order to generate the income needed to purchase portfolio insurance

The Computer Program

The computer program performs the Clean Surplus analysis on thousands of stocks. It allows you to compare all the stocks in any particular industry. This feature allows you to see at a glance the most efficient stock in each industry.

The program also allows you to separate the S&P 500 stocks from the rest of our database of stocks. This feature allows you to fill your portfolios with the best of these large- and mid-cap stocks in the same way that the test portfolios were formed in our original doctoral research. We continue to use mostly S&P 500 stocks for our model portfolios at the present time.

The original research, which resulted in continued outperformance of the S&P averages and thus 96 percent of professional money managers over any 10-year time period, used the 30 stocks from the S&P 500 stocks with the highest average of ROE over several time periods. Our computer program can perform this function for you in seconds.

This simple, easy-to-use program will be your best friend for life. Along with our weekly video newsletter, which keeps you current, you will have a full arsenal of tools to cover all aspects of your investing future.

Tutorial Videos

The easiest way to learn is through the use of visual charts, graphs, and tables accompanied with sound. Just as with our weekly video, all our tutorial videos are just that: videos with sound. In this way, you are able to sit back, rewind, fast forward, or stop and then pick up where you left off after you've come back with your second cup of coffee.

You will find a host of tutorial videos on our site under the link "Video Tutorials." We have videos that explain Clean Surplus, how to use the computer program, our dividend income and growth strategy, and our portfolio insurance strategy. Periodically, we update all of these videos as well as adding tutorial videos as you folks out there in Investment Land request them.

For Individual Investors

You may be an individual investor who can care less about spending time with research. After all, it's work and you are more efficient working at your job than structuring portfolios. You can e-mail and ask us to supply you with the names of some of the several very good money managers who follow the strategies in this book as well as the research that has been published over the past years. These money managers are able to hedge your portfolios for you and also generate the income needed to pay for those hedges.

As an individual investor, just call or e-mail us, and we'll supply you with a list of those money managers who have taken the money manager self-study course, have viewed the video, and are able to efficiently use our computer program.

For Professional Money Managers, Wealth Managers, and Investment Advisors

No professional money manager should be without the ability to effectively analyze stocks relative to a comparable operating efficiency. Clean Surplus should be the professional's first filter in the arsenal of analytical tools. After all, why would you select an inefficiently operated company over a very efficiently operated company for your clients? The answer is you wouldn't, but up to now, you probably had no idea how to determine which companies were efficient in their profit generation.

You can use our tools or we can connect you to advisors who are experts in the use of the Buffett and Beyond system. You may want to have some of your client accounts subadvised, so you don't have to worry about portfolio insurance or employing the use of enhanced income methods in order to generate income to offset the cost of the portfolio insurance. Just contact us for more information and/or the names of other money managers who are proficient in the use of Clean Surplus.

We are also able to present seminars for you and your clients in order to educate your present and future clients on the research of Clean Surplus.

In Summary: I'm Still a Teacher

So, yes, this book is just part of the whole educational organization of investor seminars, continuing professional education courses, professional money managers following our discipline, a wonderful computer program, and a host of tutorial videos.

Please remember that I'm also a university instructor. One of my goals in life is to pass on knowledge that can be used by other people to help better their lives. I want you all to make as much money as possible by investing in the best companies. If you invest in the most efficient companies, you will be reducing your risk of disappointment. The markets go up and the markets go down. We want to see your stocks go up more than the markets over the long term without taking on more risk than is generally inherent in the overall market. If you can use the information contained here and on the website to make more money than most of those around you without taking on undue risk, then I'll see you at the beach sooner than you think.

As a university instructor, I want to thank you for taking time to better your lives. After all, that's what education is all about.

About the Author

Joseph Belmonte, Ph.D, is a renowned investment strategist and market thinker. He is a stock market consultant developing hedged growth and income strategies for family offices, and he has lectured to numerous professional and investment groups throughout the country.

Dr. Belmonte has taught investments, corporate finance, and advanced managerial finance for many years both in the state university system and also in private universities throughout Florida.

He has developed several nationally sanctioned courses for CPAs, financial planners, and professional money managers. The courses for CPAs have been approved for continuing education credits in more than 38 states.

Dr. Belmonte developed a user-friendly computer program to augment the course he now teaches to professionals and serious investors. This course won acclaim from a national brokerage training school in 2013. His weekly video newsletter is sent to thousands of investors, money managers, and academics both nationally and internationally.

Index

of earnings and, 221
of growing stock, 98
increase of, 191
of stock portfolio, 190
Value Line, 26, 61–62, 75, 106, 143
Volatility, 173

Wall Street Journal, 28–29, 32
WalMart, 178, 180
www.BuffettAndBeyond.com, 2

Yearly dividend growth rate, 184–185
Yearly net income, 140